MW01225512

TWO-DOZEN BUSINESSES YOU CAN START AND RUN IN CANADA, THE USA AND ELSEWHERE

BY OBI ORAKWUE

TWO-DOZEN BUSINESSES YOU CAN START AND RUN IN CANADA, THE USA AND ELSEWHERE

BY OBI ORAKWUE

Obrake
Books
Obrake Canada Inc.
Toronto, Ontario

Copyright © by Obi Orakwue 2007

No part of this book may be reproduced and or stored in a retrieval system or transmitted in any form or by any means, electronic, mechanical, photocopying, recording, scanning or otherwise without the written authorization of the Author.

Limit of Liability/Disclaimer

At the time this edition of this book was written/published, all the phone numbers, fax numbers Websites, e-mail addresses, mailing addresses were accurate and functioning.

Although all the data and information in this book have been put through an undiscriminating and unsentimental sieve of accuracy and reliability of content, the author and publisher of this book are not liable for any disappointment, commercial, incidental and or consequential damages. You may need to consult with a professional before employing the ideas, advice and strategies contained in this book.

Book designed by Leigh Beadon.

Library and Archives Canada Cataloguing in Publication

Orakwue, Obi
    Two dozen businesse you can start and run in Canada, the USA and elsewhere / Obi Orakwue.

ISBN978-0-9782703-0-8

    1. New business enterprise--management.   I. Title.

HD62.5.0147 2007   658.1'141   C2007-900838-0

Printed in Canada by Webcom Inc., Toronto, ON

First Published in Canada in 2007
by Obrake Books
Obrake Canada Inc.
Toronto, Ontario Canada.
www.obrake.com/books

This book is dedicated to my dearest friends Echezona Santiago Orakwue, Felicia, Chinedu, Phillip and Obieze Victor. And to the hope and aspirations of all aspiring business owners.

Thanks to all the people who were interviewed
during the course of writing this book.

Table of Contents

START YOUR OWN BUSINESS
- *Why do I want to start my own business?*
- *Probable answers*
- *Why won't I start My Own Business?*
- *Probable answers*

- Advantages of Owning Your Own Business
- Disadvantages of owning your own Business

THINGS YOU NEED
- A business idea
- Expertise, Experience and Knowledge
- Features of a business plan
- Business plan resources
- Books
- Small Business Self-Help Centres
- Canadian Business Service Centres (CBSC)
- Addresses of Canada Business Service Centres by Province

START-UP CAPITAL
- Sources of Funding
- Equity
- Home Equity
- Banks
- Small Business Administration Act
- Private Individuals
- Institutional Term Lenders
- Credit Unions
- Leasing
- Accounts Receivables (Factoring)
- Venture Capital
    - o Venture Capital and Venture Capitalists of Canada
- Franchising
    - o Books on Franchising
- Government Funding
    - o Types of Government funding
    - o Government programs and services
    - o Books on Government Funding
- Books on how to Finance Your Small Business in Canada

MAKING A BUSINESS CHOICE
- Will you go for a Traditional Business or an Online Business?
- Steps For Establishing A Business Online

- What You Need To Start-Up
- Professional/Trade Associations You May Like To Join
- Books you May Need To Buy
- Other Sources Of Information
- Marketing/How To Get Business

MEDICAL/HEALTH TOURISM BUSINESS
- As medical tourism business owner, you need to know:
- What You Need To Start-Up
- Professional/Trade Associations You May Like To Join
- Books you May Need To Buy
- Other Sources Of Information
- Marketing/How To Get Business

MICROBREWERY
- As microbrewer, you need to know:
- What You Need To Start-Up
- Professional/Trade Associations You May Like To Join
- Books you May Need To Buy
- Other Sources Of Information
- Marketing/How To Get Business

TRANSLATOR/INTERPRETER
- As translator/interpreter, you need to know:
- What You Need To Start-Up
- Professional/Trade Associations You May Like To Join
- Books you May Need To Buy
- Other Sources Of Information
- Marketing/How To Get Business

ONLINE FLORIST/GIFT SHOP
- As an online florist/gift shop owner, you need to know:
- What You Need To Start-Up
- Professional/Trade Associations You May Like To Join
- Books you May Need To Buy
- Other Sources Of Information
- Marketing/How To Get Business

DATING CLUB
- As a dating club owner, you need to know:
- How Live Speed Dating works
- Online Dating
- What You Need To Start-Up
- Professional/Trade Associations You May Like To Join
- Books you May Need To Buy
- Other Sources Of Information

- Books you May Need To Buy
- Other Sources Of Information
- Marketing/How To Get Business

PUBLIC RELATIONS PROFESSIONAL/PUBLICIST
- As a publicist, you need to know:
- What You Need To Start-Up
- Professional/Trade Associations You May Like To Join
- Books you May Need To Buy
- Other Sources Of Information
- Marketing/How To Get Business

PREPAID CALLING CARDS
- As Prepaid Calling Card Business Owner, you need to know:
- What You Need To Start-Up
- Professional/Trade Associations You May Like To Join
- Books you May Need To Buy
- Other Sources Of Information
- Marketing/How To Get Business

GENERAL BRIEF ABOUT THE TWO DOZEN BUSINESSES
POINTS TO CONSIDER BEFORE CHOOSING A BUSINESS
- List of books on Marketing, Advertising and Publicity

Author's Note

Two-Dozen Businesses You Can Start and Run in Canada, USA and Elsewhere is a detailed information on 24 businesses including the general description, all you need to know before going into the business, what you need to start, the books you need to buy, trade and professional associations you need to join to enhance business networking and most importantly how to market and get business.

Research and statistics have shown time and again that more and more people wants to run their own business. This result was based on the fact that more people have realised that to make real money in this free market economy and material driven world of ours, one must stop working and making money and building other people's business empire and start making money for one's self.

However, not everybody who wants to start their own business knows the kind of business they want to start. In some cases where people know the business they want to start, they may not know where and how to start. But when exposed to different type of businesses, people tend to realize that what they think they want may not be the actual genre of their dream business.

This book is designed to expose prospective businessmen to 24 different types of evergreen businesses they may choose from. The two-dozen businesses discussed in this book, thrive throughout the year and in all seasons. A Toronto based business consultant who was consulted during the course of writing this book said thus:

'Depending on how you operate them, they could be immune to economic fluctuations and probably recession'.

All the businesses discussed in this book have the potential of developing into a multi-million dollar business. The businesses could be run as home-based businesses or office based businesses. All of the businesses could be started with less than $20,000 CDN.

More and more people are retiring, leaving corporate America, and graduating from Colleges with the sole aim of running their own show. They often search for ideas and types of business to start. This book provides two-dozen business types.

Chapter 1

START YOUR OWN BUSINESS

There are boundless opportunities to start your own business in Canada and USA.

Every minute, somebody somewhere realizes that to take control of one's professional and financial life, and make real money in a free market economy like Canada or the USA, one has to stop working one's heart out to build other people's empires and run one's own show. More people are retiring, leaving corporate America, and graduating from Colleges with the sole aim of starting and running their own businesses.

But before starting your own business, make sure you have discovered yourself. Business ownership is not for everybody. You need entrepreneurial traits and skills to be able to run a successful business. Lots of people can run a business into bankruptcy and themselves into dissatisfaction, stress and depression, but not everybody can turn a shoestring business to a multi-thousand/million dollar success that brings personal satisfaction and happiness.

Before starting your own business, answer the following questions honestly:

Why do I want to start my own business?

Probable answers include:

- **Because I like being my own boss**
  The lure of power and freedom, of being completely independent, can sometimes be overwhelming. Power and freedom are two very good things that every human being craves, but not all can handle them properly. However it is not just good enough to be a boss, you have to be a good and capable boss.

- **To make lots of money and take control of my financial life**
  It is extremely gratifying to make lots of money and enjoy all that money can buy. But remember that if you love abundance, you will never be satisfied with increase – this is good for business.

- **To escape the spell and toll of being an employee**

Your fear is rational and the trauma not unfounded. But get ready for this escape route, it could be rocky as well.

- **Because I like taking risks**

  Business in itself is always a risk, and risk taking is part of going through life. The ability to take risks is a good quality in an entrepreneur.

- **To do something different, to make a change**

  Change is inherent to human nature and environment. We live in a dynamic world, and life itself is dynamic. But change of this nature is better done when it is reasonable or necessary.

- **Because I can't find and hold a good job anywhere else**

  In life, when the desirable is unattainable, you make your attainable your desirable. But make the most out of this attainable.

- **Because I have the drive/enthusiasm**

  Although drive and enthusiasm are good traits in an entrepreneur, the two alone may not be enough to carry you through. You also need a functional plan. Like a warrior for success, your drive and enthusiasm will guide you through long hours working on your business plan.

- **Because I have a business idea/plan.**

  A good business idea, a good plan, drive and enthusiasm will carry you through to success.

- **Because I am people smart**

  Being people smart is not only to being extremely useful in business, it is also required for success in most things in life.

- **Because I have lots of common sense**

  Common sense is the basis of good sense. Most seemingly difficult and wondrous things in life were achieved using common sense. Rocket science and the science of cloning require lots of common sense. Unfortunately good sense is not always common, but common sense will play a huge factor in running a successful business.

- **Because I have trouble and liability shooting abilities**

  Both are good entrepreneurial traits that will help you resolve issues in your business as they arise.

- **Because I am very decisive and deliberate**

  The daily operation of a business involves planning, making decisions, and executing them. If you are decisive and deliberate, your business has scored a vital point in its march to success.

- **Because I am creative, original and tactful**

    Creativity, originality and tactfulness are known winners. This is another huge point for running a successful business.

Why won't I Start My Own Business?

Probable answers include:

- **Because I am afraid of uncertainties and risks involved in business**

    It is very good to be honest when identifying one's own weaknesses, provided you do not misrepresent them. But remember, there are risks in being an employee too.

- **Because I am afraid of taking complete charge and responsibility**

    Yes, starting your own business means taking total charge and total responsibility. It means taking the final decision all the way, all the time. Some people may not be comfortable with such a responsibility. But taking complete charge and responsibility of your professional and financial life means having complete freedom in your professional and financial affairs. And every human being craves freedom. So? You have to figure out what is holding you back. Do you know how and where to start?

- **Because I have no pre-knowledge of the business world**

    This sounds like one of the weakest reasons not to start your own business. In starting your own business, the most important experience you need is experience in the type of business you want to start, not necessarily the general experience of the business world.

- **Because I do not want to forgo my profession**

    You can always start a business that is related to your profession.

- **Because I am not a businessman/Entrepreneur**

    It has never been a good idea to try being what you are not. But nobody is born a businessman, people learn to become businessmen. And remember: you fail in all the things you don't try; but you stand the chance to fail and or succeed if you try. Well, you know yourself best. However, remember the following quote from Mr. Prat, the character in the factual fiction - *Overqualified Labourer*: "Although I'd never been a businessman, but I didn't allow the lack of knowledge of the business world to be a barrier".

Advantages of Owning Your Own Business

Most of the advantages of being self-employed tilt towards freedom:

- Freedom is one of the greatest cravings of all human endeavours. Starting and running your own business gives you the freedom to become the Commander-in-Chief, the Supreme Disciple of your professional and financial being.
- Starting and running your own business offers you the freedom to work at your own pace.
- Managing your own business gives you the freedom to make your decisions as you deem fit.
- Owning a business means there will be no Boss breathing down your neck all the time
- The glory of success in the business is all yours.
- If you build an empire out of the shoestring business, it's all yours.
- You don't work your heart out to build someone else's empire.

Disadvantages of owning your own Business

Most of the disadvantages of owning a business tilt towards the price of freedom:
- Freedom, like most things in life, has it's own price
- Being your own Commander-in-Chief also means being liable for all failures in the business.
- Taking all the glory for success also means taking all the blame for failure.
- You work long hours for all profits and losses.
- Being a boss may be more stressful than being an employee.

Chapter 2

The primary things you need to start and run a successful business include:

- **A business idea**

  It always start with an idea, a brilliant and viable idea. As a prospective business owner who needs to be in control of your professional and financial destiny, your idea needs to be related to your profession and skills, and it needs to target a particular audience. Conduct all the necessary research on your idea as it relates to this economy and market. The next step will be to develop a plan based on the results of the research. In conducting your research, use the resources that are available like the library, bookstores, yellow pages and directories, trend books, magazines and newspapers, research studies, Internet, interviewing people and cold calls.

  Have a look at the Book:
  Look Before You Leap: Market Research Made Easy
  Published By Self-Counsel Press
  Author: Don Doman, Dell Dennison & Magaret Doman
  ISBN: 0-88905-292-8

- **Expertise, Experience and Knowledge that relates to the business venture you are about to undertake**

  If your business idea tilts towards your profession, skill or trade, then you already have the expertise, the experience and knowledge of the business venture you are undertaking. It makes things easier than going into an area where you are a novice.

- **A business plan**

  Remember the advantages of planning.
  Your business plan will dissect, assemble, structure and direct your business idea. Depending on how you want to finance your business, potential investors will vet your business plan before investing. It is therefore necessary to have a detailed business plan.

Features of a business plan Include:

o   Executive Summary
o   A business name
o   Business/Company Objectives
o   Business Overview
o   Business Ownership
o   Workers Hierarchical Structure
o   Management
o   Mission Statement
o   Products and Services
o   Operations
o   Location of Business Premise
o   Capital equipment
o   Competitors / Competition
o   SWOT Analysis–Strength, Weakness, Opportunities, Threats (Risks)
o   Start-up Requirements
o   Success Strategy
o   Marketing/Advertising and Publicity Strategy
o   Action Plan
o   Financial Plan
o   Start-up Requirements
o   Addendum

For help on how to write a business plan, use the following resources:

- The Library
- Websites:
    o   www.planmaker.com
    o   www.pasware.com
    o   www.sba.gov/shareware/starfile.html
    o   www.jianusa.com
    o   www.planet-corp.com
    o   www.brs-inc.com
    o   www.smartonline.com
- Books
    Preparing a Successful Business Plan
    By Rodger D. Touchie
    Self-Counsel Press
    ISBN: 1-55180177-9

    Rules Book of Business Plans For Start-Up: Create a Winning Plan That You Can Take To The Bank
    Published by Entrepreneur Press
    Author: Roger Rule
    ISBN: 1-932531-05-X

Business Plan For Dummies
Published by Wiley Publishing Inc.,
Author: Tiffany Paul
ISBN: 1-56884-868-4

The Business Planning Guide
Published by Dearborn Trade Publishing
Author: David H. Bangs, Jr
ISBN: 079315409-X

Business Plans Kit For Dummies
Published by Wiley Publishing Inc.,
Author: Steven Peterson
ISBN: 076455365-8

- Small Business Self-Help Centres
  Small business self-help centres offer advice and guidance to people starting their own businesses, and to people who already have their business up and running. The advice, information and guidance they offer includes: writing a business plan, financing a business, business management, and general assistance.

Start-Up Capital

Sometimes entrepreneurs with a good business idea and an excellent business plan do not have enough funds to start their business. As such, they have to depend on other people's money. When approaching a financial institution for a start-up loan, the bait you need is a good business plan and an excellent loan proposal.

Sources of Funding:
- **Equity**
  This is the term used to represent the money that you and probably your partner(s)/associate(s) put into the business.
- **Home Equity**
  The equity in your home is the difference between the appraised value of your home and your current mortgage balance. You can use your home equity as collateral security if you need to borrow money.
- **Banks**
- **Small Business Administration Act**
  All Chartered Banks and Alberta Treasury branches are authorized to advance loans under the Small Business Administration Loans Act.
- **Private Individuals**
- **Institutional Term Lenders**
- **Term lending is available from:**
- **Most Chartered Banks**
- **Credit Unions**
- **Business Development of Canada (BDC)**

- **Credit Unions**
- **Leasing**
- **Accounts Receivable (Factoring)**
- **Venture Capital**

  For more information on Venture Capital and Venture Capitalists of Canada contact:

  Canada Venture Capital Association
  234 Eglinton Avenue East
  Suite 200
  Toronto, On
  M4P 1K5
  Phone: 416-487-0519
  Website: www.cvca.ca

- **Franchising**

  For more information on Franchising, Contact:

  Canadian Franchising Association
  2585 Skymark Avenue, Suite 300
  Mississauga, On
  L4W 4L5
  Phone: 905-625-2896
  Toll Free: 1-800-665-4232
  Fax: 905-625-9076
  Website: www.cfa.ca

  Or:

  International Franchise Association
  1350 New York Avenue N.W., Suite 900
  Washington, D.C. 20005-4709
  Phone: 202-628-8000
  Website: www.franchise.org

  Books on Franchising

  Franchising in Canada
  Published by Self-Counsel Press
  Author: Michael Coltman
  ISBN: 1-55180-094-2

  A Guide for Franchisors and Franchisees, Business, Taxation and Accounting Issues
  Published by: CCH Canada limited
  Author: Taylor Gilbert, David Thompson and Peter Dabbikeh
  ISBN: 1-55141-755-3

  Franchising: A Complete Guide for Canadian Buyers and Sellers
  Published by: Key Porter Books
  Author: Bev Cline

ISBN: 1-55013-113-3

- **Government Funding**

  Government financial assistance for Small Business in Canada is an unsentimental, unbiased form of business funding. It may be very time consuming, involves lots of paper work, but it is a good source of financial assistance to start up a small business, and to support a business that is already in operation.

  Types of Government funding:
  - Cash grants
  - Management Assistance
  - Loan guarantees
  - Reduced interest rates
  - Subsidies

  For more information about Government funding, programs and services, see the following:

  Business Development of Canada (BDC)
  Phone: 1-800-INFO-BDC (1-800-4636-232)
  Website: www.bdc.ca

  Reference Canada
  They provide information about all Federal Government Programs and Services for Small Business.
  Phone 1-800-667-3355

  Export Development of Canada
  Corporate Communications Department
  Export development of Canada
  151 O'Connor Street
  Ottawa, On
  K1A 1K3
  Phone: 613-598-2500
  Toll Free: 1-800-575-4422
  Website: www.edc.ca

  Books on Government Funding

  Handbook of Grants and Subsidies
  Published by Canadian Research and Publication Centre
  Author: Canadian Research and Publication Centre
  ISBN: 2892120519

Government Programs and Services
Published by Employment and Immigration Canada
Author: Canada Employment and Immigration (Commission)
ISBN: 0662591194

Your Guide To Government Of Canada Services And Support For Small Business
Published by Government of Canada
ISSN: 1209-0069

Your Guide to Government of Canada Services and Support for Small Business
Published by Industry Canada
Author: Industry Canada
ISBN: 0662251539

Your Guide To Government Of Canada Services And Support For Small Business
Published by Government of Canada
Author: Entrepreneurship and Small Business Office
ISBN: 0662251539

Sources of Small Business Funding in Canada
Published by Entrepreneurial Business Consultants of Canada
Author: Entrepreneurial Business consultants of Canada

Government Assistance for Canadian Business
Published by Carswell
Author: Prudhomme Donna, Singer Ronald, and Roy Robert
ISBN: 0459573462

The Canadian Reference Directory on Business Planning and Financing
Published by The Canadian Sources of Funds Index
Author: The Canadian Sources of Funds Index

The Canadian Business Assistance Handbook
Published by The Canadian Institute of Chartered Accountants (CICA)
Author: CICA

Your Guide To Government Financial Assistance For Business in Ontario
The latest details of all Federal, Provincial and other Assistance Programs that relate to enterprise in Ontario
Published by Productive Publications

Author: Iain Williamson
ISBN: 1-55270-133-6
ISSN: 1198-0524

Canadian Industrial Incentives Legislation
Published by Butterworths

Industrial Assistance Programs in Canada
Published by CCH Canada Ltd.
Author: Horsley David, David Bramwell
ISBN: 0887965628

Government Assistance Programs in Canada: Practical Handbook
Published by CCH Canada
Author: Huras Lorraine, Miller Peter, Peat Marwick Thorne
ISBN: 0887968228

Your Guide to Government Financial Assistance in Ontario
Published by: Productive Publications
Author: Iain Williamson
ISSN: 1198-0524

Your Guide to Government Financial Assistance in Quebec
Published by: Productive Publications
Author: Iain Williamson
ISSN: 11980540

Your Guide to Start Up Financing in Canada
Published by: Productive Publications
Author: Iain Williamson
ISBN: 0920847080 V1
0920847099 V2
0920847102   V3
0920847072 V3.set

Or you can visit any of the following centres:

Canadian Business Service Centres (CBSC)
CBSC is found in every province. In the province of Quebec, it is called Info Entrepreneurs. The centres provide information on:
o   Financial assistance program
o   Starting a business
o   Regulatory requirements
o   Taxation
o   Trade and export opportunities
Website: www.cbsc.org

Email: cobsc@cbsc.ic.gc.ca

Addresses of Canadian Business Service Centres by Province:

Canada/Ontario Business Call Centre
Toronto, Ontario
M5V 3E5
Phone: 416-954-INFO (4636)
Toll Free: 1-800-240-4192
Website: www.cbsc.org/ontario/index.html
Email: cobcc@cbsc.ic.gc.ca

Canada/British Columbia Business Service Centre
601 West Cordova Street
Vancouver, British Columbia
V6B 1G1
Phone: 604-775-5525
Toll Free: 1-800-667-2272
Fax: 604-775-5515
Toll Free Fax: 1-800-667-2272
Email: olson.dave@cbsc.ic.gc.ca (For Business Start Up)
    marcarenhas.carm@cbsc.ic.gc.ca (For Trade and Markets/Export-Import)
Website: www.sb.gov.bc.ca/small-bus/sbhome.html

Alberta - The Business Link
Business Service Centre
Ste. 100, 10237-104 Street
Edmonton, Alberta
T5J 1B1
Phone: 403-422-7722
Toll Free: 1-800-272-9675
Fax: 403-422-0055
Info-Fax: 403-427-7971
Toll Free Fax: 1-800-563-9926
Website: www.cbsc.org/alberta/index.html
Email: buslink@cbsc.ic.gc.ca

Canada/Nova Scotia Business Service Centre
1575 Brunswick Street
Halifax, Nova Scotia
B3J 2G1
Phone: 902-426-8604
Toll Free: 1-800-668-1010
Fax: 902-426-65-30
Info-Fax: 902-426-3201

Toll free: 1-800-401-3201
TTY: 1-800-797-4188
Email: halifax@cbsc.ic.gc.ca
Website: www.cbsc.org/ns/index.html

Quebec - Info Entrepreneurs
5 Place Ville Marie
Niveau Plaza, Suite 12500, Plaza Level
Montreal, Quebec
H3B 4Y2
Phone: 514-496-4636
Toll Free: 1-800-322-4636
Fax; 514-496-5934
Info Fax: 514-496-4010
Toll free: 1-800-401-3201
TTY: 1-800-887-6550
Email: info-entrepreneurs@bfdrq-fordg.gc.ca
Website: www.cbsc.org/org/quebec/index.html

Manitoba - Canada Business Service Centre
330 Portage Avenue, 8th Floor
P.O.BOX 2609
Winnipeg, Manitoba
R3C 4B3
Phone: 204-984-2272
Tool Free: 1-800-665-2019
Fax: 204-983-3852
Info Fax: 204-984-5527
Toll free: 1-800-665-9386
Email: manitoba@cbsc.ic.gc.ca
Website: www.cbsc.ic.gc.ca

Canada/New Brunswick Business Service Centre
570 Queen Street
Fredericton, New Brunswick
E3B 6Z6
Phone: 506-444-6140
Tool Free: 1-800-668-1010
Fax: 506-444-6172
Info Fax: 506-444-6169
Toll free: 1-800-401-3201
TTY: 1-800-887-6550
Email: cbscnb@cbsc.ic.gc.ca
Website: www.cbsc.org/nb/index.html

Newfoundland - Canada Business Service Centre
90 O'Leary Avenue

P.O.BOX 8687
St. John's, Newfoundland
A1B 3T1
Phone: 709-772-6022
Toll Free: 1-800-668-1010
Fax: 709-772-6090
Toll free: 1-888-772-6030
Email: St.johns@cbsc.ic.gc.ca
Website: www.cbsc.org/nfld/index.html

Canada/Northwest Territories Business Service Centre
P.O.BOX 1320
8th Floor Scotia Centre
Yellowknife, Northwest Territories
X1A 2L9
Phone: 867-873-7958
Toll Free: 1-800-661-0599
Fax: 867-873-0575
Toll free: 1-800-661-0825
Email: yel@cbsc.ic.gc.ca
Website: www.cbsc.org/nwt/index.html

Canada/Saskatchewan Business Service Centre
122-3rd Avenue, North
Saskatoon, Saskatchewan
S7K 2H6
Phone: 306-956-2323
Toll Free: 1-800-667-4374
Fax: 306-956-2328
Info Fax: 306-956-2310
Toll free: 1-800667-9433
Email: saskatooncsbsc@cbsc.ic.gc.ca
Website: www.cbsc.org/sask/index.html

Canada/Prince Edward Island Business Service Centre
75 Fitzroy Street
P.O.BOX 40
Charlettown, Prince Edward Island
C1A 7K2
Phone: 902-368-0771
Toll Free: 1-800-668-1010
Fax: 902-566-7377
Info Fax: 902-368-0776
Toll free: 1-800-401-3201
TTY: 902-368-0724
Email: pei@cbsc.ic.gc.ca

Website: www.cbsc.org/pei/index.html

Canada/Yukon Business Service Centre
201-208 Main Street
Whitehorse, Yukon
Y1A 2A9
Phone: 867-633-6257
Toll Free: 1-800-661-0543
Fax: 867-667-2001
Info Fax: 867-633-2533
Toll free: 1-800-841-4320
Email: perry.debbie@cbsc.ic.gc.ca

For information on how to Finance Your Small Business in Canada see the Books:

Where To Go When The Bank Says No
Financing your Small Business in Canada
Published by McGraw-Hill Ryerson Limited
Author: Gary Fitchett
With John Alton
Kathleen Aldridge
ISBN: 0-07-560225-3

When The Banks Says No
Creative Financing for Closely Held Business
Published by Liberty Hall Press
Author: Lawrence W. Tuller
ISBN: 0-8306-3590-4

Starting A Successful Business in Canada
16th Edition
Published by Self-Counsel Press
Author: Jack D. James
ISBN: 1-55180-573-1

Your Guide To Government Financial Assistance
For Business in Ontario
The latest details of all Federal, Provincial and other Assistance Programs that relate to enterprise in Ontario
Published by Productive Publications
Author: Iain Williamson
ISBN: 1-55270-133-6
ISSN: 1198-0524

- **Be a Businessman/Entrepreneur**

  Being a Businessman/Entrepreneur is quite different from being an employee. As a businessman, you have to breathe, eat, drink, sleep and dream your business. You have to be prepared for it.

Chapter 3

MAKING A BUSINESS CHOICE

When choosing a business, you must choose a business that has to do with the things you enjoy doing. As a prospective business owner, professional and or a skilled tradesperson, it is assumed that you enjoy your chosen area of interest, profession, and skill, and as such it is advisable that you choose a business that is somewhat related to your area of interest, chosen profession and skill.

Whatever business you choose to establish, it is advisable to establish a business in the things you enjoy doing. Imagine making money doing what you most enjoy. Fun, eh? Real fun.

Will you go for a Traditional Business or an Online Business?

Traditional business means non-virtual business, non-internet-based business. Online Business means businesses conducted on the Internet/World Wide Web.

One good thing about the online business is that, depending on how your Website is designed, nobody knows how big or small your business is. You can be whatever you want to be on the Internet.

The process of establishing an online business or a traditional business is almost the same, except for a few steps that sets starting an online business apart from a traditional business.

Steps for Establishing a Business Online:

- Establish a relationship with a courier company who will be responsible for delivering your products to your customers.
  Some courier companies:
  - Canada Post
  - UPS
  - TNT
  - DHL
  - FEDEX

  For local (within the city) deliveries, you may arrange with efficient local dispatchers to be more cost effective.
- Find an Internet Service Provider (ISP) for your Internet services

- Create a website and employ the services of Internet/computer programmers, writers, graphic artists and photographers.
- Obtain a merchant account so you can to accept credit card payment online.
- Ensure that your website can process a secure financial transaction. Security is the greatest concern for people who do business online.

Merchant accounts could be obtained from banks and financial institutions.
For examples of where to obtain a merchant account, see the websites:

o   **Merchant Account Company** - www.merchantaccount.com
o   **USB Merchant Services** - www.creditcards-atm.com
o   **Merchant Express** - www.merchantexpress.com
o   **Keycorp Merchant Services** - www.keybank.com
o   **Secure-Bank.Com**
o   **Electronic Transfer, Inc** - www.paymentmall.com
o   **Harris Bankcard Centre** - www.harrisbank.com/smallbusiness/merchant/cihome.html
o   **Credit Merchant Account Services** - www.merchantaccount.net
o   **EPD Credit Card Services** - www.apc.net/edp/cc.html
o   **https://backoffice.merchantmanager.com**
o   **First American Card Services** - www.1stamericancardservice.com/basefold.html

- **For more information on how to start an online business see the books:**

The Unofficial Guide to Starting a Business Online
Published by Wiley Publishing, Inc.
Author: Jason R. Rich
ISBN: 0-02-863340-7

Doing Big Business on the Internet
Published by Self-Counsel Press
Author: Hurley & Birkwood
ISBN: 1-55180-119-1

Selling On The Web
Author: Paul Galloway
ISBN: 1563824876

Start an eBay Business
Published by Alpha Books
Author: Barbara Weltman
ISBN: 159257-333-9

Small Business Online
A Strategic Guide for Canada Entrepreneurs
Published by Prentice Hall Canada Inc.,
Author: Jim Carroll with Rich Broadhead
ISBN: 0-13-976895-5

101 Ways To Promote your Website
Published by Maximum Press
Author: Susan Sweeney
ISBN: 1931644217

Start Your Own Business On eBay: Your Step by Step Guide To Success
Published by Entrepreneur Press
Author: Jacquelyn Lynn
ISBN: 1932531122

Start Your Own E-Business
Published by Entrepreneur Press
Author: Entrepreneur Press
ISBN: 1932156747

Selling On The Net: The Complete Guide
Published by NTC Business Books
Author: Lewis, Herschell Gordon
ISBN: 0844232343

Selling On The Internet: How to Open an Electronic Storefront and Have Millions of Customers Come to You
Published by McGraw-Hill
Author: James C. Gonyea, Wayne M. Gonyea
ISBN: 0070241872

The Online Business Book
Published by Adam Media Corporation
Author: Rob Liflander
ISBN: 158062-3204

Guerrilla Marketing Online
Published by Houghton Mifflin
Author: Jay Conrad Levinson and Charles Rubin
ISBN: 0-395-86061-X

Internet Marketing For Dummies
Published by Wiley Publishing Inc.,
ISBN: 0-7645-0778-8

Low-Cost Website Promotion
Published by Adam Media Corporation
Author: Barry Feig
ISBN: 1-58062-501-0

Online Business Resources
Published by Made E-Z
Author: Paul Galloway
ISBN: 1-56382-510-4

Generating Trust in Online Business: From Theory To Practice
Published by IQ
Author: Magda Fusaro
ISBN: 2-922417-28-X

Absolute Beginner's Guide To Launching an eBay Business
Published by Que
Author: Michael Miller
ISBN: 0-7897-3058-8

Starting an eBay Business For Dummies
Published by Wiley Publishing Inc.,
Author: Marsha Collier
ISBN: 0-7645-6924-4

Online Business Planning
Published by Career Press
Author: Robert T. Gorman
ISBN: 1-56414-369-4

Chapter 4

YOUR BUSINESS STRUCTURE

In Canada, businesses are differentiated into structures using the following Terms:

Proprietorship

This form of business structure involves only one person. It is the simplest and easiest form of business to start. In this form of business, the assets of the business owner and the assets of the business are inseparable. It is a one-in-all, all-in-one type of thing. The actions of the proprietor while conducting business bind the business and the actions/activities of the business bind the proprietor. You and your assets are liable to everything that goes wrong - taxes, debts, lawsuits, etc. in the business. The business dies with the death of the proprietor.

Partnership

This form of business structure is one step ahead of the proprietorship structure of business. It involves two or more persons who, out of free will, enter into an agreement/partnership to undertake a business venture for the purpose of generating profit, with each partner entitled to a certain capital contribution and share of profit.

There is a Provincial Partnership Act in every province in Canada that governs the Partnership Business.

All partners are liable to the losses, taxes, debt and lawsuits that may be incurred by the business. In other words, Partnership is about the same as Proprietorship, except that in a Partnership, you have more than one person sharing the profits and or liabilities of the business. And the business does not die with the death of one partner, but with the death of all the partners.

In a Partnership, a lot of trust, confidence and faith is required among the partners, because the excesses of one partner in the conduct of the business binds the other partners of the business.

Corporation

This type of business structure involves two or more people bound by a Memorandum of Association/Articles of Incorporation. It is a limited liability company - meaning that the business is a separate legal entity from the owners of the business. As such, the owners (shareholders) of the company are not liable for the company's debt, losses, and lawsuits above their capital contributions for share ownership in the company. The company often outlives the owners (shareholders).

There are three types of Corporation:

- C- Corporation
- S-Corporation
- Limited Liability

Ask your Lawyer/Accountant about the tax advantages of each type of corporation and incorporation process/procedure. Your lawyer will also clarify issues about licenses, permits, insurance, laws and regulations with regards to you and your business.

For more information on incorporation of a company see the books:

Start A Successful Business in Canada
Published by self-Counsel Press
Author: Jack D. James
ISBN: 1-55180-573-1

Incorporation and Business Guide
Published by Self-Counsel Press
Author: M. Stephen Georgas
ISBN: 1-55180-219-8

Starting a Business: A Complete Guide to Starting and Managing Your Own Company
Published by Key Porter Books Limited
Author: Gordon Brockhouse

Start Your Own Business: The Canadian Entrepreneur's Guide
Published by Stoddart Publishing Company Limited
Author: Peter D. Cook

The Complete Canadian Small Business Guide
Published by McGraw-Hill Ryerson
Author: Douglas A. Gray and Diana Lynn Gray
ISBN: 0-07-086495-0

Small Business Success: A Practical Guide for the Entrepreneur
Published by CCH Canadian Limited
Author: Tony Fattal

Vault Reports Guide To Starting Your Own Business
Published by Houghton Mifflin Company
Author: Jonathan Reed. Aspatore with H. S. Hamadeh, Samer Hamadeh & Mark

Oldman
ISBN: 0-395-86170-5

Building a Dream: A Canadian Guide To Starting Your Own Business
Published by Mcgraw-Hill Ryerson
Author: Walter S. Good
ISBN: 0-07-086271-0

Starting on a Shoestring : Building a Business Without a Bankroll
Published by John Wiley & Sons, Inc.
Author: Arnold S. Goldstein
ISBN: 0-471-23288-2

The Complete Canadian Small Business Guide
Published by McGraw Hill
Author: Douglas Gray and Diana Gray
ISBN: 007086495-0

You may also like to visit the following offices:

Ministry of Industry, Trade and Technology
Hearst Block
900 Bay Street (7th Floor)
Toronto, Ontario
M7A 2E1
Phone: 416-965-5494
Toll Free: 1-800-387-6142

Small Business Development Corporation
Ministry of Revenue
33 King Street West
Oshawa, Ontario
L1H 8H9
Phone: 416-434 -7232

Your Business Image

Your image on paper and or in person must be right for business - clean and simple. Do it to impress, make no mistakes about it. Your image in person and on paper is part of your business product, and it must be packaged excellently.

In person, you need a briefcase and a business suit. You need to be "people smart" - smile, pay attention and listen to people, and address people by their names.

On paper, you need a letterhead, a logo, good business card, a brochure and mailing labels. All of them go a long way towards making you appear like the professional you are.

The Office

As a new business owner, depending on your type of business, you must choose an office according to the resources at your disposal. You may like to have a commercial space, an executive office suite, a shared space, a subleased space or you may choose to run your business from your home. Running a business from home is the most cost-efficient.

In your office you must have:
- Computer
- Printer
- Photocopy machine
- Fax machine
- Scanner
- Phone

...or you can just get a computer with Internet connection, a phone line, and an all-in-one machine that faxes, copies, scans, and prints.

Your Computer

Use a desktop or a laptop computer with a 56k modem. Install the following software in the computer:

- **Word processor (MS Office) -** Use this to write letters, create mailing labels, and address envelopes. In the MS Office you've got MS Word, Excel, Access, Outlook, and PowerPoint.
- **Spreadsheet** - You can create charts and do your finances with a spreadsheet program. Use MS Excel for your spreadsheet needs.
- **QuickBooks Pro** - With this, you can create custom invoices, compute sales, do electronic banking, pay your bills, control your inventory and payroll. Use it for all accounting and bookkeeping.
- **Database** - Use a database program to keep records of clients, sellers, vendors and all your business contacts/links. With the database program, you can keep records of phone calls, faxes, meetings, conferences and seminars, and note time and dates of events and incidents. You may want to use MS Access, Dbase or Fox Pro for your database needs.
- **Graphic** - Use this to create flyers, announcements newsletters and advertisements. You may want to use PageMaker, QuarkXpress and ClarisWorks for your graphic exploits.
- **Scheduler** - Use this to manage your schedules.

Your Phone

Look and Sound Big and Professional Using Phone System Tricks. Call Bell Canada and or Sprint Canada to inquire about calling packages. You must have the following features to operate smoothly:

- **Voice Mail**

    Choose a group voice mail where the callers/clients will select from a list of names and departments in the company by pressing the appropriate numbers on their touch tone phone as directed by your outgoing message.

Use a good and professional voice to record your outgoing message. You may employ the services of a friend who has a good and professional voice, or you can employ the services of a professional.

An example of a professional out going message is:

"Hello, you have reached the administrative office of The BIZ Company. We are sorry that we are unable to take your call at this moment. We are either on another line or assisting other clients. If you leave your name and your phone number and a brief message, someone will get back to you as soon as possible."

As seen in the above message, always use 'we' when referring to your company. Never use 'I' even though you may be running the company alone. By using the plural 'we', you give the impression that the company is a big company with many employees, and that you are not running the company alone.

- **Caller Display/Caller ID with name**
  This feature allows you to see the telephone number of the caller and probably know who is calling before answering the phone.

- **Call Waiting**
  This feature allows you while on a line with a person, to keep this person on one line, while receiving another incoming call. But if you identify the incoming caller using the caller display, you may choose to ignore him/her if need be, and your voice mail will answer the phone.

- **Ring Mate/Ring Tones**
  Ringmate/Ringtone allows you the freedom of using two phone numbers (Home/Business) on one line, thereby saving you the extra cost of paying for another line. In using the ring mate feature, your two phone numbers ring on the same phone line but with different tones. The different ring tones allow you to know which phone number is being called and how to answer it.

- **Call Transfer/Forwarding Feature**
  If you are not home and or in the office, but must attend to a particular call, the call transfer feature allows you to forward the call to your office phone and or to your cell phone. But this doesn't need to happen often.

- **Fax Switch Box**
  With a fax switch box, you can connect your fax machine to your phone line, and when a call comes in, the switch box differentiates and directs the call to the right section.
  Three-way Calling

For furniture, Home office equipment and other office basics, visit the office supply superstore in your area:

- Staples
- Home Depot
- Wal-Mart.

Some Trade/Business Associations

CANADA

The Toronto Board of Trade
Downtown Centre
1 First Canadian place
P.O.Box 60
Toronto, Ontario
M5X 1C1
Phone: 416-366-6811
Fax: 416 366-8406
Website: www.bot.com

Association of Independent Consultants
15 Wilson Street
Markam, Ontario
L3P 1M9
Phone: 416-410-8163
Fax: 905-294-9435
Email: info@aiconsult.ca
Website: www.aiconsult.ca

Canadian Chamber of Commerce
350 Sparks St., suite 501
Ottawa, Ontario
K1R 7S8
Phone: 613-238-4000
Fax: 613-238-7643
Website: www.chamber.ca

Canadian Federation of Independent Business
4141 Yonge St., Suite 401
Willowdale, Ontario
M2P 2A6
Phone: 416-222-8022
Fax; 416-222-7593
Website: www.cfib.ca

Canadian Organization of Small Business Inc.
#102, 100101-107 A Avenue
Edmonton, Alberta
T5H 4H8
Phone: 403-423-2672
Fax: 403-423-2751

Direct Sellers Association
190 Attwell Drive, Suite 630
Etobicoke, Ontario
M9W 6H8
Phone: 416-679-8555
Fax: 416-679-1568
Website: www.dsa.ca

International Organization for Entrepreneurs
32 Tollerton avenue
North York, Ontario
M2K 1H3
Phone: 416-202-8310
Toll free: 1-877-482-0236
Fax: 416-202-8310
Website: www.ioe.org

Inventors' Alliance of Canada
47 Kenneth avenue
Toronto, Ontario
M6P 1J1
Phone: 416-410-7792
Fax: 416-762-3301

The Canadian Federation of Independent Grocers
2235 Sheppard Avenue east, suite 902
Willowdale, Ontario
M2J 5B5
Phone: 416-492-2311
Toll free: 1-800-661-2344
Fax: 416-492-2347

Women Entrepreneurs of Canada
1630 Ewald Road
Mississauga, Ontario
L5G 4C3
Phone: 416-388-5586
Fax: 905-274-5366
Email: wec@wec.ca

Website: www.wec.ca

Young Entrepreneurs Association
1209 King St., West, suite 205
Toronto, Ontario
M6K 1G2
Phone: 1-888-639-3222
Fax: 1-888-639-7969
Email;Toronto@yea.ca
Website: www.yea.ca

Canadian Marketing Association
Phone: 416-391-2362
Fax: 416-441-4062
Website: www.the-cma.org

Associations Canada 2005
20 Victoria St.
Toronto, Ontario
M5C 2N8
Phone: 416-362-5211
Toll free: 1-800-387-2689
Fax: 416-362-6161
Email: info@micromedia.on.ca
Website; www.micromedia.on.ca

This is the directory of all associations in Canada.

Better Business Bureau
Check website for regional locations
www.bbb.org

USA

National Business Association (NBA)
P.O.Box 700728
Dallas, Texas 75370
Phone: 972-458-0900
Toll free: 1-800-456-0440
Fax; 972-960-9149
Email: info@nationalbusiness.org
Website: www.nationalbusiness.org

U.S. Chamber of Commerce
1615 H Street, NW

Washington, DC 20062-2000
Phone: 202-659-6000
Toll free: 1-800-638-6582
Website: www.uschamber.com

New York Board of Trade
World Financial Centre
One North End Avenue, 13th floor
New York, NY 102882
Phone: 212-748-4000: 212-748-4094
Toll free: 1-800-HEDGE-IT
Email:marketing@nybot.com
Website: www.nybot.com

Empire State Development
Division for Small Business
30 south Pearl street
Albany, NY 12245
Phone: 1-800-STATE NY
        1-800-782-8369
Website: www.nylovessmallbiz.com

California Small Business Association
P.O.Box 661235
Los Angeles, CA. 90066
Phone: 1-800-350-CSBA
Fax: 310-642-0849
Email: csba@pacbell.net
Website: www.csba.com

Business Marketing Association
410 N. Michigan Ave., Suite 1200
Chicago, IL 60611
Phone: 1-800-664-4BMA
Fax: 312-822-0054
Website: www.marketing.org

Direct Marketing Association (DMA)
1120 Avenue of the Americas
New York, NY 10036-6700
Phone: 212-768-7277: 212-790-1500
Fax: 212-302-6714
Email: customerservice@the-dma.org
Website: www.the-dma.org

Institute of Management Consultants USA, Inc.
2025 M Street NW, Suite 800
Washington, DC 20036-3309
Phone: 202-367-1134
Fax; 202-367-2134
Email: tbgrp@mindspring.com
Website: www.imcusa.org

Independent Management Consultants of Sacramento (IMC USA)
IMC USA Management Consultants of Sacramento
3525 Eastern Avenue
Sacramento, CA 95821
Phone: 916-359-7238
Fax: 916-359-7239
Email: imcsacto@aol.com
Website: www.sacramentconsultants.org

American Marketing Association
311 South Wacker Drive, Suite 5800
Chicago, IL 60606
Phone: 1-800-AMA-1150
Fax: 312-542-9000: 312-542-9001
Website: http://appserver.marketingpower.com

USA Packaging Gateway Industry, governmental and related organizations in USA
Packaging-Gateway.com
Website: www.packaging-technology.com

USA Business Directory

Business Directory of USA
www.businessdirectoryofusa.com

Reference USA
www.referenceusa.com
InfoUSA Library Division
5711 S. 86th Circle
P.O.Box 27347
Omaha, NE 68127
Phone: 1-800-808-1113

Response USA
www.responseusa.com
3 Executive Campus

Cherry Hill, New Jersey 08002
Phone: 1-856-661-0700

Chapter 5
TWO DOZEN BUSINESSES YOU CAN RUN IN CANADA, THE USA AND ELSEWHERE

Business Broker/ Business Brokerage Firm

When Individuals, Companies, Businesses, and Organizations, big, medium and small, want to buy and or sell a business, they turn to Business brokers, because it is more effective – faster and more convenient.

As a Business Broker, you will be matchmaking buyers and sellers of businesses. You will be helping buyers and sellers to buy, sell, locate and merge with businesses that meet their needs.

Nowadays, many people leave Corporate Canada and Corporate America with a dream of starting their own business in order to take control of their own professional and financial life. The baby boomers are retiring and selling off their businesses. More people are relocating than ever. The business of Business Brokerage is booming.

You will be representing the buyer and or seller on a commission basis of between 5% - 15%, and retainer fees.

You may want to specialize in buying and selling businesses under one-million dollars or above one-million dollars.

Examples may include: Restaurants, coffee shops, fitness centres, service businesses, retail/convenience stores, supermarkets, yachts, transport businesses, gas stations, delivery businesses, dry cleaning businesses, house/office cleaning businesses, taverns, manufacturing businesses, factories, automotive service centres, printing shops, distribution companies, wholesale companies, packaging businesses, etc.

They could be of any size.

As a business broker, you need to know:

- **Marketing** – Marketing skills are an indispensable feature of a good businessman
- **Strategy** – It is a known winner
- **People-smartness** – In the business of matchmaking, people-smartness is indispensable
- **Business Evaluation** – You have to evaluate a business properly to be able to

put a price tag on it

- **Industry and market trends** – This knowledge will be invaluable during the process of evaluation
- **Economic growth cycles** – Good knowledge of this will help in evaluating, forecasting and advising your clients
- **Competition** – Knowledge of the competitors of the business being sold or purchased will be of invaluable help
- **History and profit trends of businesses** – History and trends greatly influence the future
- **Viability of locations and facilities** – Location and facility is a very important factor when buying or selling a business
- **Risk associated with each business** – Evaluating the risk of a business somehow means knowing the worth of the business
- **Inventory** – You evaluate a business with the inventory of the business
- **Letters of intent** – To be provided by the business owner to show proper reason and motivation for selling
- **Procurement of loans and funds** – Sometimes, you may help you clients secure a loan and the funds he needs to purchase the business
- **Price negotiation** – You must be able to conduct an effective negotiation
- **Legal terms of buying and selling** – You must be able to cope with the legalities of business transactions
- **Affiliation with a lawyer** – Helps in preparing the purchase and sale agreement, and gives legal spicing to the whole transaction
- **Knowledge of business immigration laws/ Affiliation with an immigration lawyer** – Sometimes you may be helping foreign investors to purchase a business and qualify for a business visa
- **Purchase and sale agreement** – The final stage of the transaction before funds change hands

What You need To Start-Up

- A Computer (with Internet connection)

Use a desktop or a laptop computer with a 56k modem. Install the following software on the computer:

- o **Word processor (MS Office) -** Use this to write letters, create mailing labels, and address envelopes. In the MS Office you've got MS Word, Excel, Access, Outlook, and PowerPoint.
- o **Spreadsheet** - You can create charts and do your finances with a spreadsheet program. Use MS Excel for your spreadsheet needs.
- o **QuickBooks Pro** - With this, you can create custom invoices, compute sales, do electronic banking, pay your bills, control your inventory and payroll. Use it for all accounting and bookkeeping.
- o **Database** - Use a database program to keep records of clients, sellers, vendors and all your business contacts/links. With the database program, you can keep records of phone calls, faxes, meetings,

conferences and seminars, and note time and dates of events and incidents. You may want to use MS Access, Dbase or Fox Pro for your database needs.

o **Graphic** - Use this to create flyers, announcements newsletters and advertisements. You may want to use PageMaker, QuarkXPress and ClarisWorks for your graphic exploits.

o **Scheduler** - Use this to manage your schedules.

- Phone, Fax, Printer, Scanner, Copier (can buy all-in-one)
- Office Furniture (including office supplies and office accessories)
- Insurance
- Fees payable to become a member in professional and or trade associations.
- Books
- Marketing/advertising cost.
- Business suits, ties, shoes, briefcase (all for personal image improvement) and other miscellaneous expenses

Professional/Trade Associations You May Like To Join

Better Business Bureaus:

Better Business Bureau of Mid-Western and Central Ontario
Website: www.bbbmwo.ca
Email: info@bbbmwo.ca
Phone: (519) 579-3080
Fax: (519) 570-0072
354 Charles Street East
Kitchener, Ontario
N2G -4L5

BBB of Mainland British Columbia
Website: www.bbbvan.org
Email: inquiries@bbbvan.org
Phone: (604)-682-2711
Fax: (604) 681-1544
404-788 Beatty Street
Vancouver, British Columbia
V6B -2M1

BBB of Central & Northern Alberta
Website:www.edmontonbbb.org
Email: info@edmontonbbb.org
Phone: (780)-482-2341
Fax: (780)-482-1150
#888 Capital Place, 9707 - 110 Street
Edmonton, Alberta
T5K -2L9

The Vancouver Board of Trade
World Trade Centre
Suite 400, 999 Canada Place
Vancouver, British Columbia
V6C 3E1
Phone: 604-681-2111
Fax: 604-681-0437
E-mail: contactus@boardoftrade.com
Website: www.boardoftrade.com
Website: www.vancouver.boardoftrade.com

- **Ontario Business Brokers Association**
- **Western Canada Business Brokers Association**
- **Canadian Real Estate Association**
- **Alliance for Business Brokers and Intermediaries**
- **Canadian Franchise Association**

Institute of Business Appraisers
P.O. Box 17410 - Plantation
FL 33318
Phone: 954-584-1144
Fax: 954-584-1184
e-mail: ibahq@go-iba.org
Website: www.go-iba.org

New York Association of Business Brokers
Institute of Certified Business Counselors
18615 Willamette Drive
West Linn, OR 97068
Phone: 877.icbc.org (877.422.2674)
Fax: 503.292.8237
Website: www.cbc.org
General information: inquiry@i-cbc.org
Membership: membership@i-cbc.org

International Business Broker Association
IBBA Headquarters
401 North Michigan Avenue
Suite 2200
Chicago, Illinois 60611-4267
Phone: 888.686.IBBA (4222)
Fax: 312.673.6599
Website: www.ibba.org
E-mail: admin@ibba.org

Books you May Need to Buy:

Complete Guide to Business Brokerage
By Tom West
Third Edition

How to Avoid 101 Small Business Mistakes, Myths and Misconceptions (Paperback)
By Gary L. Shine

In and Out of Business
By Toedore P. Burbank

Buying a Business Made Easier
BLUE BOOK OF CANADIAN BUSINESS
By International Press Publications, Inc.
90 Nolan Court, # 21 Markham, Ontario
L3R 4L9
Tel: 1-800-679-2514 or (905) 946-9588
Fax: (905) 946-9590

- **Information on yacht brokers**
- **Buying and selling boat tips**
  Yacht broker certification and membership.
- **Website: www.bcmta.com/bcyba/**

Marketing/How To Get Business

Hunting for business for your Brokerage firm is about the same as searching for job or a contract. As such, you have to apply all the job/contract search skills you have learnt over the years, customizing them to suit your present need and position.

- Cold calls to companies, businesses, organizations, etc. for information interviews about who wants to buy/sell what.
- Make contact with the trade division of Embassies and Consulates of foreign
- Countries for buying/selling leads in their countries.
- Visit Chambers of Commerce
- Networking
- Resumes
- Brochure/Flyers
- Business Cards
- Create a Website
- Join Associations/Social Clubs
- Trade Fairs

Chapter 6

CONSULTING

The field of consulting is as wide as the oceans. It is growing even wider and will never stop growing. Consultants have sprang up in fields like Rocket Science, Gene Therapy, Cloning, Engineering, Business, Military, Dating, People Smartness, Marital Harmony, Hair Styling and Nail Polishing. There is no aspect of human endeavour where consultants have not pitched their flags.

As a consultant, you need the following skills:

- Problem solving
- People smart
- Cross-examination
- Imagination, Instinct and intuition of a Psychologist
- Instincts to develop leads
- Trendy
- Pro-active
- Specificity
- Research skills
- Ability to read extensively, including magazines, journals, publications and newsletters

But above all you need:

- Knowledge, Expertise and Experience.

Your consultancy firm is like an oracle, and you as the consultant, are the supreme priest. As a consultant you dispense advice, clarification, and lasting solutions to the problems, confusions, and difficulties of your clients, be them Governments, Companies, Organizations and or individuals.

The usefulness of knowledge, expertise and experience is not knowledge, expertise and or experience in themselves, but their application to resolve issues and achieve success. As a consultant, you need to know how to apply specific knowledge, expertise and experience to a specific problem to achieve a specific solution.

You are a professional with knowledge, expertise and years of experience.

Having spent years in formal training, years of work experience with the practical application of your knowledge and expertise, you have the core things it takes to be a consultant in your field. What are you waiting for? Rise to the bait and join the razzle.

Be a consultant in your own field!

What You need To Start-Up

- A Computer (with Internet connection)

    Use a desktop or a laptop computer with a 56k modem. Install the following software on the computer:
    - **Word processor (MS Office)** - Use this to write letters, create mailing labels, and address envelopes. In the MS Office you've got MS Word, Excel, Access, Outlook, and PowerPoint.
    - **Spreadsheet** - You can create charts and do your finances with a spreadsheet program. Use MS Excel for your spreadsheet needs.
    - **QuickBooks Pro** - With this, you can create custom invoices, compute sales, do electronic banking, pay your bills, control your inventory and payroll. Use it for all accounting and bookkeeping.
    - **Database** - Use a database program to keep records of clients, sellers, vendors and all your business contacts/links. With the database program, you can keep records of phone calls, faxes, meetings, conferences and seminars, and note time and dates of events and incidents. You may want to use MS Access, Dbase or Fox Pro for your database needs.
    - **Graphic** - Use this to create flyers, announcements newsletters and advertisements. You may want to use PageMaker, QuarkXpress and ClarisWorks for your graphic exploits.
    - **Scheduler** - Use this to manage your schedules.
- Phone, Fax, Printer, Scanner, Copier (can buy all-in-one)
- Office Furniture (including office supplies and office accessories)
- Insurance
- Fees payable to become a member in professional and or trade associations.
- Books
- Marketing/advertising cost.
- Business suits, ties, shoes, briefcase (all for personal image improvement) and other miscellaneous expenses

The total cost of your start-up needs will not exceed $20,000 Canadian.

Professional/Trade Associations You May Like To Join:

Canadian Association of Management Consultants
BCE Place
181 Bay Street
P.O.BOX 835

Toronto, Ontario
M5J 2T3
Phone: 416-860-1515
Website: www.camc.com

The Toronto Board of Trade
Downtown Centre
1 First Canadian place
P.O.Box 60
Toronto, Ontario
M5X 1C1
Phone: 416-366-6811
Fax: 416 366-8406
Website: www.bot.com

Canadian Chamber of Commerce
350 Sparks St., suite 501
Ottawa, Ontario
K1R 7S8
Phone: 613-238-4000
Fax: 613-238-7643
Website: www.chamber.ca

Canadian Federation of Independent Business
4141 Yonge St., Suite 401
Willowdale, Ontario
M2P 2A6
Phone: 416-222-8022
Fax; 416-222-7593
Website: www.cfib.ca

Canadian Organization of Small Business Inc.
#102, 100101-107 A Avenue
Edmonton, Alberta
T5H 4H8
Phone: 403-423-2672

Better Business Bureau
Check website for regional locations
www.bbb.org

Books You May Need To Buy:

Start and Run a Profitable Consulting Business
Published by Self-Counsel Press

Author: Douglas A. Gray
ISBN: 1-55180-106-X

How to Become a Successful Consultant in Your Own Field
Published by Prima Publishing
Author: Hubert Bermont
ISBN: 0761511008

The Complete Guide To Consulting Success
Published by Upstart Publishing
Author: Ted Nicholas, Howard L. Shenson, and Paul Franklin
ISBN: 1574100556

Consulting For Dummies
Published by IDG Books Worldwide
Author: Bob Nelson and Peter Economy
ISBN: 0764550349

Marketing Your Consulting and Professional Services
Published in New York by John Wiley & Sons
Author: Dick Connor, Jeffrey P. Davidson, and Richard A. Connor
ISBN: 0471133922

Consultant & Independent Contractor Agreements
Published by Nolo Press
Author: Stephen Fishman
ISBN: 0873374576

How to Be Your Own Publicist
Published by McGraw-Hill
Author: Jessica Hatchigan
ISBN:0-07-138332-8

6 Steps To Free Publicity
Published by Career Press Inc
Author: Marcia Yudkin
ISBN: 1-56414-675-8

Guerrilla Publicity
Published by Adams Media Corporation
Author: Jay Conrad Levinson, Rich Frishman and Jill Lublin
ISBN: 1-58062-682-3

Marketing Without Advertising
Author: Michael Phillips, Salli Rasberry
ISBN: 0873376080

Other sources of information include:
- Seminars
- Magazines
- Journals
- Newsletters
- Trade Publications
- Websites

Marketing/How To Get Business

Hunting for business for your consultancy firm is about the same thing as searching for a job/contract in your field of interest. As such, you have to apply all the job search skills you have acquired over the years, customizing them to suit your present need and position.

- Cold Calls (for information interviews)
- Networking
- Resumes
- Brochures/Flyers
- Business Cards
- Create a Website
- Associations/Social clubs
- Trade Fairs

Good luck!

Chapter 7

CUSTOMS BROKERAGE FIRM/CUSTOMS BROKER

A Customs Broker can be an individual, a partnership of individuals, a firm, or a Corporation.

When Importers decide not to engage in the process of clearing their own imported goods, they may choose to employ the services of a Customs Brokerage Firm/Customs Broker and authorize them to clear their goods.

Customs Brokerage Firms therefore prepare required documents for the clearing of imported and exported goods on behalf of their clients – importers/exporters. They act as liaison/facilitator between the importer and the government department. In doing so, the Customs Brokerage Firm ensures that the clients adhere to the rules and guidelines as stipulated in the government legislature, and minimize the client's exposure to Administrative Monetary Penalties (AMPS).

In order for a Customs Brokerage Firm or a Customs Broker to be able to manage the clearing, documentation, accounting and payment of duties for imported goods, the firm or individual must be licensed by the Canada Border Services Agency (CBSA).

The CBSA Licensing Regulations recommend:

- **Before Licensing**
    - o Application Procedures
    - o Qualification Requirements
    - o Professional Examinations
- **After Licensing**
    - o Record Keeping Procedures
    - o Provisions for Renewing, Suspending and Canceling a License
    - o Terms and conditions of the License

The Customs Brokers Professional Examination

This examination is conducted by the Canada Customs and Revenue Agency (CCRA), to ensure that Custom Brokers have sufficient knowledge of the rules, regulations, policies and procedures regarding the importation and exportation of goods before they are deemed fit to be Licensed.

See Section 15 of the Customs Brokers Licensing Regulations.
Memorandum D1-8-1, Licensing of Customs Brokers.

The Customs Brokers Professional Examinations are conducted at least once a year in all regions. Prospective candidates may apply to sit for the examination at any site of their choice. Prospective candidates must apply using Form L55, Application for Customs Brokers Examination. The completed application form must be submitted in duplicate to the nearest CCRA office, at least 30 days before the examination date. The application must be accompanied by a non-refundable fee made payable to the Receiver General for Canada.

For More Information, Contact:

Brokers Licensing and Account Security Programs
Import Process Division
Canada Customs and Revenue Agency
8th Floor, Sir Richard Scott Building
191 Laurier Avenue West
Ottawa, Ontario
K1A 0L5
Phone: 613-941-4789
Fax: 613-946-0242
Toll free (information): 1-800-461-9999
Toll free (publication): 1-800-959-2221
Website: www.cbsa-asfc.gc.ca/

As a Customs Broker, you need to have the knowledge of:
- The Customs Act, the Customs Tariff, the Excise Act, the Excise Tax Act, and the Special Import Measures Act
- CCRA regulations, policies, and procedures relating to the reporting and release of goods and the accounting and payment of duties
- CCRA legislation as regards the importation and exportation of goods
- CCRA regulations as regards establishment and operation of customs brokerage offices
- General business accounting practices
- Copies of the Customs Act, the Customs Tariff, the Excise Act, the Excise Tax Act, the Special Import Measures Act, and the CCRA directives could be obtained from:
  Canadian Government Publishing
  Room 1309A
  45 Sacré-Coeur Boulevard
  Hull QC K1A 0S9
  Telephone: (819) 956-4802
  Toll Free: 1-800-635-7943

What You need To Start-Up

- A Computer (with Internet connection)

  Use a desktop or a laptop computer with a 56k modem. Install the following software on the computer:
    o **Word processor (MS Office) -** Use this to write letters, create mailing labels, and address envelopes. In the MS Office you've got MS Word, Excel, Access, Outlook, and PowerPoint.
    o **Spreadsheet** - You can create charts and do your finances with a spreadsheet program. Use MS Excel for your spreadsheet needs.
    o **QuickBooks Pro** - With this, you can create custom invoices, compute sales, do electronic banking, pay your bills, control your inventory and payroll. Use it for all accounting and bookkeeping.
    o **Database** - Use a database program to keep records of clients, sellers, vendors and all your business contacts/links. With the database program, you can keep records of phone calls, faxes, meetings, conferences and seminars, and note time and dates of events and incidents. You may want to use MS Access, Dbase or Fox Pro for your database needs.
    o **Graphic** - Use this to create flyers, announcements newsletters and advertisements. You may want to use PageMaker, QuarkXpress and ClarisWorks for your graphic exploits.
    o **Scheduler** - Use this to manage your schedules.
- Phone, Fax, Printer, Scanner, Copier (can buy all-in-one)
- Office Furniture (including office supplies and office accessories)
- Insurance
- Fees payable to become a member in professional and or trade associations.
- Books
- Marketing/advertising cost.
- Business suits, ties, shoes, briefcase (all for personal image improvement) and other miscellaneous expenses

Professional/Trade Associations You May Like To Join/Know:

Customs Brokers Association Of Canada
85 Albert St, Ottawa, Ontario

The Canadian Society of Customs Brokers
320, 55 Murray Street
Ottawa, Ontario
K1N 5M3
Telephone: 613-562-3543
Facsimile: 613-562-3548
Email: cscb@cscb.ca (for general inquiries)
Email: ccs@cscb.ca (for Certified Customs Specialists inquiries)

Website: www.cscb.ca

International Federation of Customs Brokers Associations
55 Murray Street Street
Suite 320
Ottawa, Ontario
K1N 5M3
Canada
E-mail: ifcba@ifcba.org
Website: www.ifcb.org

Canadian Chamber of Commerce
350 Sparks Street, Suite 501
Ottawa, Ontario K1R 7S8
Tel: (613) 238-4000
Fax: (613) 238-7643

Canadian Council for International Business
350 Sparks Street, Suite 501
Ottawa, Ontario
K1R 7S8
Tel: (613) 230-5462
Fax: (613) 230-7087

Canadian Importers Association Inc.
210 Dundas Street West Suite 700
Toronto, Ontario
M5G 2E8
Tel: (416) 595-5333
Fax: (416) 595-8226

Alliance of Manufacturers and Exporters Canada
75 International Boulevard, 4th floor
Etobicoke, Ontario
M9W 6L9
Tel: (416) 798-8000
Fax: (416) 798-8050

The World Customs Organization
Belgium
Tel: 00 32 (0) 2 209 95 03
Fax: 00 32 (0) 2 209 94 90
Email: www.wcoomd.org

Books and Publications You May Need to Read:

Canadian Government Publishing
Room 1309A
45 Sacré-Coeur Boulevard
Hull QC K1A 0S9
Telephone: (819) 956-4802
Toll Free: 1-800-635-7943

WCO - Publications Department
Rue du marché, 30
B-1210 Brussels
Belgium
Tel : 00 32 (0)2 209 95 03
Fax : 00 32 (0)2 209 94 90
E-mail : publications@wcoomd.org
Email: www.wcoomd.org/ie/en/bookshop.html

A Basic Guide to Importing
Published by Lincolnwood, 111, USA: NTC Business Books
Author: US Customs Service
ISBN: 0844234036 (pbk)

Export/Import Procedures and Documentation
Published by AMACON
Author: Thomas E. Johnson
ISBN: 0814403506 or 081440734

Other Sources of Information:

Administrative Monetary Penalty System (AMPS)
www.cbsa-asfc.gc.ca
Canada Customs Tariff
www.cbsa-asfc.gc.ca/general/publications
Canada Customs Technical Notices
www.cbsa-asfc.gc.ca/general/publications
Canada International Trade Tribunal
www.citt-tcce.gc.ca/index
Canadian Society of Custom Brokers
www.cscb.ca
Customs D Memoranda
www.cbsa-asfc.gc.ca/menu
Department of Foreign affairs
www.dfait-maeci.gc.ca
Finance Canada
www.fin.gc.ca/fin
Industry Canada
http://strategie.ic.gc.ca/

Natural Resources Canada
www.nrcan.gc.ca
Revenue Canada
www.rc.gc.ca
- For useful information regarding importing into Canada, taxation, and general goods and services tax.
- Access to the latest Customs and taxation bulletins

Apec Tariff
www.apectariff.org
- Information about any APEC member country like Japan and other useful trading information

Canada Business Network
http://canadabusiness.gc.ca/
Canadian Trade Commissioner Service
http://infoexport.gc.ca.
Team Canada
www.tcm-mec.gc.ca
Trade Negotiations and Agreements
www.dfait-maeci.gc.ca
NAFTA Secretariat - Canadian Section
www.nafta-sec-alena.org
Team Canada Inc
http://exportsource.ca

Marketing/How To Get Business

Hunting for business for your Brokerage firm is about the same as searching for job/contract. As such, you have to apply all the job search skills you have acquired over the years, customizing them to suit your present need and position.
- Cold calls to manufacturers for information and interviews about who wants to export/import what.
- Make contact with the trade division of Embassies and Consulates of foreign Countries for export/import leads in their countries.
- Visit Chambers of Commerce
- Networking
- Resumes
- Brochure/Flyers
- Business Cards
- Create a Website
- Join Associations/social clubs
- Trade fairs

Chapter 8

DOG BAKERY BUSINESS

Nowadays, people are more conscious of what they eat than ever. People want and tend to eat more natural and organic product than processed foods laden with chemical, additives and preservatives. This trend will improve the health and wellness of the human populace. However, this trend is slowly being extended to man's best friend – the dog. The regular pet foods from the regular pet stores are loaded with chemicals, preservatives, additives, processed sugars, colouring, fillers, meat-by-products, etc. Undoubtedly, feeding our dogs with mass-processed pet foods affects their behaviour, attitude, physical well-being and general health.

By owning and running a dog bakery, you will not only be partaking in a billion dollar industry, but you will also be participating in the revolution for a natural way to feed our best four-legged friends.

A dog bakery is a low-risk, virgin niche market and a fun business one can start and run from anywhere in and around Canada and the USA.

As a dog Bakery Business owner, you need to have:
- Passion for pets
- Interest in baking
- Basic baking skill
- Interest in the natural way of feeding
- Knowledge of legalities involved with baking dog / pet treats
- Ingredients for treats
- Mould prevention
- Types of gourmet goodies
- Recipes for dogs
- Veterinarian approved ingredients
- Knowledge of the latest trend in organic dog treats

- Imagination
- Test dogs

What You need To Start-Up

- A Computer (with Internet connection)

  Use a desktop or a laptop computer with a 56k modem. Install the following software on the computer:
  - o **Word processor (MS Office)** - Use this to write letters, create mailing labels, and address envelopes. In the MS Office you've got MS Word, Excel, Access, Outlook, and PowerPoint.
  - o **Spreadsheet** - You can create charts and do your finances with a spreadsheet program. Use MS Excel for your spreadsheet needs.
  - o **QuickBooks Pro** - With this, you can create custom invoices, compute sales, do electronic banking, pay your bills, control your inventory and payroll. Use it for all accounting and bookkeeping.
  - o **Database** - Use a database program to keep records of clients, sellers, vendors and all your business contacts/links. With the database program, you can keep records of phone calls, faxes, meetings, conferences and seminars, and note time and dates of events and incidents. You may want to use MS Access, Dbase or Fox Pro for your database needs.
  - o **Graphic** - Use this to create flyers, announcements newsletters and advertisements. You may want to use PageMaker, QuarkXpress and ClarisWorks for your graphic exploits.
  - o **Scheduler** - Use this to manage your schedules.
- Phone, Fax, Printer, Scanner, Copier (can buy all-in-one)
- Office Furniture (including office supplies and office accessories)
- Insurance
- Fees payable to become a member in professional and or trade associations.
- Books
- Marketing/advertising cost.

Professional/Trade Associations You May Like To Join/Know:

Canadian Dog Clubs

Canadian Kennel Club
89 Skyway Avenue, Suite 100
Etobicke, ON
M9W 6R4
Phone: 416-675-5511
Toll free: 1-800-250-8040
Fax: 416-675-6506
Email: information@ckc.ca

Website: www.ckc.ca

The German Shepherd Dog Club of Canada

Canadian Eskimo Dog Club of Canada
C/o Laura Pitblado-Kelly
RR # 2
Huntsville, Ontario
P1H 2J3
Website: www.canadianeskimodog.com

Canadian Animal Health Network
Website: www.cahnet.org

- **Veterinary Medical Association**
- **Animal Rights Group**
- **Council of Dogs Club**
- **National Association of Dogs Club**
- **Pet Owners Association**

Books You May Need To Buy:

Barker's Grub : Easy, Wholesome Home-Cooking for Dogs (Paperback)
By Rudy Edalati

Real Food for Dogs: 50 Vet-Approved Recipes to Please the Canine Gastronome
By Arden Moore

Better Food for Dogs: A Complete Cookbook and Nutrition Guide
By David Basin

Three Dog Bakery Cookfood
By Beckloff

Homemade Treats for Happy Dogs
By Cheryl Gianfrancesco

Dr. Pitcairn's Complete Guide to Natural Health for Dogs & Cats
By Richard H. Pitcairn

The Consumer's Guide to Dog Food: What's in Dog Food, Why It's There and How to Choose the Best Food for Your Dog
By Liz Palika

How to Have a Healthier Dog: the Benefits of Vitamins and Minerals for Your Dog's Life Cycles
By Wendell O. Belfied

The Good Food Cookbook For Dogs: 50 Home-Cooked Recipes for the Health and Happiness of Your Canine Companion
By Donna Twichell Roberts

Throw me a bone: 50 Healthy, Canine Taste-Tested Recipes for Snacks, Meals, and Treats
By Sally Sampson

Home- Prepared Dog & Cat Diets: The Healthy Alternative
By Donald R. Strombeck

Start Your Own Dog Bakery Business – Book

Some Useful Links:
- www.zukes.com
- www.mymommybiz.com
- www.healthyhoundbakery.com
- www.dogchefs.com
- www.k9treat.com
- www.dogthymetreats.com
- www.bakeadogabone.com
- www.bakbytes.com

Marketing/How To Get Business

Hunting for business for your Dog Bakery Business is about the same as searching for a job. As such, you have to apply all the job search skills you have learnt over the years, customizing them to suit your present need and position.
- Cold calls to dog owners, dog clubs, pet associations for information and interviews about who wants a better feeding plan for his/her pet.
- Visit Pet Associations
- Attend local pet event.
- Networking
- Resumes
- Brochure/Flyers
- Business Cards
- Create a Website
- Join Associations/Social clubs
- Trade Fairs
- Veterinary Offices
- Pet Stores
- Kennels

- Dog Daycare centres
- Flea Markets
- Press Release
- Newsletters

Good luck!

Chapter 9

EVENT AND MEETING PLANNING BUSINESS / EVENT CONSULTANT

Lots of names have been employed in the effort to define this business in the most appropriate way, because of the vast area it covers. Names like Event Planner, Event Consultant, Event manager, Event Planning Coordinator, Event Planning Professional etc.

Nowadays, when friends, families, companies, and organizations want to organize a big, medium or small party or event, they employ the services of an event planner. This is because they may not have the time, expertise, resources or ability to organize the event to an expected standard in this our increasingly socially and politically correct society.

As an event planner, you will be organizing events, meetings, rally, ceremony etc for your clients to a financially, socially and or politically required/accepted standard.

The things you require as an event planner may include:

- Be an extrovert
- Have high energy level
- Be organized
- Multi-tasking ability
- Great attention to detail
- Ability to work under pressure
- Be very creative
- Be a fast thinker
- Have self-motivation
- Be a good motivator
- Trouble shooting skills
- Problem solving skills
- Be people smart
- Good communication skills
- Supervisory skills
- Abillty to work with people from different socio-cultural and economic backgrounds

- Team player/leader
- Be bondable and flexible
- Good negotiation techniques
- Execution tactics
- Be research oriented
- Good sense of entertainment
- Very trendy
- Good sense of fashion
- Coordinating ability
- Ability to evaluate events
- General knowledge of logistics and operation
- Excellent networking ability
- Lots of experience
- If possible, obtain a degree/diploma/certificate in event planning and or event management.

In a case you decide to obtain a certification, you may check with the following organizations:

International Special Events Society – they offer Certified Special Events Professional (CSEP)
Website: *www.ises.com/csep*
Meeting Professionals International – they offer Certification in Meeting Management (CMM)
Website: *www.mpiweb.org/education*
Convention Industry Council – they offer Certified Meeting Professional Program (CMP) Certificate
Website: *www.conventionindustry.org/cmp*
Connected International Meeting Professionals Association – they offer Certified Global Meeting Planner Certificate
Website: *www.cimpa.org/cgmp*
Association of Destination Management Executives – they offer Destination Management Certified Professional Certificate
Website: *www.adme.org*

The Event planning business is a billion industry with a wide-cast niche.

Areas of specialization include:

Corporate Events
Corporate events are events hosted by Businesses, Organizations, Companies, Corporations, Political Parties and Government. The events could be trade fairs/shows, art exhibitions, seminars, symposiums, conferences, fashion fairs/shows, shareholders meetings, executive and board meetings, gala nights, book and product launching, inauguration parties, political rally, etc.

Social Events

Social events are events like musical concerts, weddings, civic events, birthday celebrations, parties, memorials, graduations, etc.

You may choose to specialize in one or more of the areas mentioned above.

What You need To Start-Up

- A Computer (with Internet connection)

    Use a desktop or a laptop computer with a 56k modem. Install the following software on the computer:
    - **Word processor (MS Office) -** Use this to write letters, create mailing labels, and address envelopes. In the MS Office you've got MS Word, Excel, Access, Outlook, and PowerPoint.
    - **Spreadsheet** - You can create charts and do your finances with a spreadsheet program. Use MS Excel for your spreadsheet needs.
    - **QuickBooks Pro** - With this, you can create custom invoices, compute sales, do electronic banking, pay your bills, control your inventory and payroll. Use it for all accounting and bookkeeping.
    - **Database** - Use a database program to keep records of clients, sellers, vendors and all your business contacts/links. With the database program, you can keep records of phone calls, faxes, meetings, conferences and seminars, and note time and dates of events and incidents. You may want to use MS Access, Dbase or Fox Pro for your database needs.
    - **Graphic** - Use this to create flyers, announcements newsletters and advertisements. You may want to use PageMaker, QuarkXpress and ClarisWorks for your graphic exploits.
    - **Scheduler** - Use this to manage your schedules.
    - **Event Planning Software**
        - Event Planner Plus from Certain Software
        - MeetingPOWER, Optimum Settings and STS Resorts Express from PC/Nametag.
        - Marketing Pilot Software for Event Planners
- Phone, Fax, Printer, Scanner, Copier (can buy all-in-one)
- Office Furniture (including office supplies and office accessories)
- Insurance
- Fees payable to become a member in professional and or trade associations.
- Books
- Marketing/advertising cost.
- Business suits, ties, shoes, briefcase (all for personal image improvement) and other miscellaneous expenses

Professional/Trade Associations You May Like To Join/Know:

Independent Meeting Planners Association of Canada - IMPAC
52 Lowe Blvd
New market, Ontario
L3Y 5T1
Phone: 905-868-8008
Fax: 905-895-1630
Email: impac@impaccanada.com
Website: www.impaccanada.com

International Special Events Society - ISES

ISES CANADA
www.isescanada.com
Toronto Chapter
www.isestoronto.com
Vancouver Chapter
www.isesvancouver.com
Calgary Chapter
www.isescalgary.com

Convention Industry Council - CIC
CIC Headquarters Office
8201 Greensboro Drive, Suite 300
McLean, VA 22102 USA
Phone: 1 (703) 610-9030
Fax: 1 (703) 610-9005
Website: www.conventionindustry.org

Financial & Insurance Conference Planners
Head Office:
401 N. Michigan Ave.
22nd Floor
Chicago, IL 60611
Phone: (312) 245-1023
Fax: (312) 321-5150

Canadian Region
Kelly Porter
Manulife Financial - (519) 747-7000
kelly_porter@manulife.com
Website: www.ficpnet.com

ICCA - International Congress & Convention Association
ICCA North America

Ms. Joanne H. Joham
Regional Manager North America
Box 323
US- Summit, New Jersey 07902-0323
Phone: +1 908 233 8635
Fax: +1 908 233 8636
Website: www.iccaworld.com

Meeting Professionals International
Toronto, Ontario
Phone: 416- 504-9777
Website: www.mpitoronto.org

Professional Convention Management Association
2301 South Lake Shore Drive
Suite 1001
Chicago, IL 60616-1419
USA
Phone: 1- 312-423-7262
Fax: 1-312-423-7222
Toll-free: 1-877-827-7262
Website: www.pcma.org

PCMA Canada
Ontario
Phones: 416- 860-6814, or 416- 597-1400
Website: www.pcma.org

British Columbia
> **Tourism Vancouver**
> #210, 200 Burrard St.
> Vancouver, British Columbia
> V6C 3L6
> Phone: (604) 631-2881
> Fax: (604) 682-1717
> Website: www.pcma.org

Books You May Need To Buy:

How to Start and Run a Home-Based Event Planning Business
By Jil Moran.

Event Planning: The Ultimate Guide to Successful Meetings, Cooperate Events, Fundraising Galas, Conferences, Conventions, Incentives and Other special Events.
By Judy Allens

Opportunities in Event Planning Careers
By Blythe Camenson

The Essential Event Planning Kit
By Godfrey Harris

Fabjob Guide to Become a Wedding Planner
By Catherine Goulet

Start Your Own Event Planning Business: Your Step-by-Step Guide to Success
By Krista Turner

The Business of Event Planning: Behind-the-Scene Secrets of Successful Special Events
By Judy Allen

Complete Idiot's Guide to Meeting and Event Planning
By Robin E. Craven

Event Planning Ethics and Etiquette: A Principled Approach to the Business of Special Event Management
By Judy Allen

Meeting & Event Planning for Dummies
By Susan Friedmann

Plan a Fun Conference
By Karen Wheless

Plan a Conference, Retreat or Event
By Angela Yee

Marketing/How To Get Business

Hunting for clients for your Event Management Business is about the same as searching for a job in your field. As such, you have to apply all the job search skills you have learnt over the years, customizing them to suit your present need and position.

- Cold calls to Companies, Businesses, Schools, Organizations and Events/Conference/Convention Organizers for information and interviews about who may need the services. Provide them with reasons they may need the services of your Event Management Firm.
- Find out and incorporate the marketing methods and approaches of other professionals in your field into your own method and approach.
- Network with other professionals in your professional Organization

- Participate in company meetings, chamber of commerce activities, professional organizations, networking with everybody at any given opportunity.
- Yellow Pages advertisement
- Brochure/Flyers
- Business Cards
- Create a Website
- Associations/social clubs
- Distribute gift certificates and discount event packages to clients to give to their friends
- Send out event planning package offers for special days and seasons like Christmas New Year, Easter, Canada Day, Valentine's Day etc.
- Keep in touch with your clients and call the clients who have not used your services for some time to remind them of your good services, new leads and discounted offers that are available.
- Call your clients - new/old/regular, weeks, months and or years after they use your services to thank them for using the services of your event management firm, but above all, to ask them how they are doing and how satisfied they are with the result of the earlier event management.
- Offer free event management to your regular clients for referrals - if they bring in four or more new clients.
- Develop a weekly/monthly newsletter, write in the local newspaper and or magazine giving tips on how to increase awareness, and excellent event management. Act like the professional you are.

Good luck!

Chapter 10

EXPORT/IMPORT AGENT

Many Canadian companies both big and small, are in constant need of the knowledge and connections of an independent export/import agent to sell/buy their goods - raw materials, semi-finished and or finished products and components abroad.

You can fill this niche and undertake the exportation/importation of goods and or services from any country/global region of origin to and from Canada. You can become a commissioned agent, in which case you make a commission on any sale you make for the company/manufacturer. On the other hand, you can become a retainer agent, and be paid a fixed amount of money to work for a company/manufacturer for a particular product over a particular period of time.

As an Export/Import agent, you need to have:

- Knowledge of Export/Import procedures and documentation
- Knowledge of the government procedures (Canadian/your home government and the countries you will be doing business in)
- Knowledge of goods that require export/import license
- Methods of guaranteeing payments
- Knowledge of letters of credit (revocable, irrevocable, transferable and non-transferable letters of credit)
- Knowledge of custom procedures
- Knowledge of Export/Import Financing
- Knowledge of culture/language

What You need To Start-Up

- A Computer (with Internet connection)

    Use a desktop or a laptop computer with a 56k modem. Install the following software on the computer:
    - **Word processor (MS Office) -** Use this to write letters, create mailing labels, and address envelopes. In the MS Office you've got MS Word, Excel, Access, Outlook, and PowerPoint.
    - **Spreadsheet** - You can create charts and do your finances with a

spreadsheet program. Use MS Excel for your spreadsheet needs.
- o **QuickBooks Pro** - With this, you can create custom invoices, compute sales, do electronic banking, pay your bills, control your inventory and payroll. Use it for all accounting and bookkeeping.
- o **Database** - Use a database program to keep records of clients, sellers, vendors and all your business contacts/links. With the database program, you can keep records of phone calls, faxes, meetings, conferences and seminars, and note time and dates of events and incidents. You may want to use MS Access, Dbase or Fox Pro for your database needs.
- o **Graphic** - Use this to create flyers, announcements newsletters and advertisements. You may want to use PageMaker, QuarkXpress and ClarisWorks for your graphic exploits.
- o **Scheduler** - Use this to manage your schedules.
- o **Event Planning Software**
  - Event Planner Plus from Certain Software
  - MeetingPOWER, Optimum Settings and STS Resorts Express from PC/Nametag.
  - Marketing Pilot Software for Event Planners
- Phone, Fax, Printer, Scanner, Copier (can buy all-in-one)
- Office Furniture (including office supplies and office accessories)
- Insurance
- Fees payable to become a member in professional and or trade associations.
- Books
- Marketing/advertising cost.
- Business suits, ties, shoes, briefcase (all for personal image improvement) and other miscellaneous expenses

Professional/Trade Associations You May Like To Join/Know:

Canadian Exporters Association
99 Bank Street,
Suite 250
Ottawa, Ontario
K1P 6B9
This body has Regional Offices across Canada

Canadian Importers Association
438 University Avenue
Suite 1618
P.O.BOX 60
Toronto, On
M5G 2K8
Phone: 416-595-5333
Website: www.importers.ca
This Association offers seminars for their new members - 'Import Canada'

The Alliance of Manufacturers and Exporters Canada
1 Nicholas Street,
Suite 1500
Ottawa, On
K1N 7B7
Phone: 613-238-8888
Website: www.cme-mec.ca

5995 Avesbury Road
Suite 900
Mississauga, Ontario
L5R 3P9
Phone: 905-568-8300

75 International Boulevard,
Suite 400
Toronto, On
M9W 6L9
Phone: 416-798-8000
Fax: 416-798-8050

Ontario Association of Trading Houses
Website: www.oath.on.ca

Quebec Association of Export Trading Houses
Website: www.amceq.org

Canada Custom and Revenue Agency
This agency has a useful information service for would-be importers/exporters.
Contact them at:
    Ontario
    Great Toronto Area (GTA)
    Phone: 416-952-0114
    ACIS: 1-800-461-2096
    English: 1-800-461-9000
    French: 1-800-952-2036

    Ottawa -Phone: 613-991-0537
    Windsor-Phone: 519-257-6355
    Hamilton- Phone: 905-308-8605
    London- Phone: 519-645-5843

Team Canada Inc.
Phone (Toll Free): 1-888-811-1119

Books You May Need To Buy:

Exporting from Canada
Published by Self-Counsel Press
Author: Gerhard W. Kautz
ISBN: 1-55180-342-9

Your Guide To Canadian Export Financing
Author: Iain Williamson

Export-Import Financing
Author: M. Venedikian

Documentary Letters of Credit
Published by The International trade Services of Bank of Nova Scotia. It is also available through their Website: www.scotiabank.ca/trade/index.html

Export Manager: Guide to Export marketing and Management
Published by XPO International
Author: Morris NG
ISBN: 0-9698593-0-9
A Basic Guide to Exporting
Published by World Trade Press
Author: Woznick Alexander
ISBN: 1885073844
        1885073836(pbk)

A Basic Guide to Importing
Published by Lincolnwood, 111, USA: NTC Business Books
Author: US Customs Service
ISBN: 0844234036 (pbk)

Export/Import Procedures and Documentation
Published by AMACON
Author: Thomas E. Johnson
ISBN: 0814403506 or 081440734

Profitable Exporting: A Complete Guide To Marketing your Product Abroad
Published by Willey
Author: John S. Gordon, J.R. Arnold
ISBN: 0-471-61334-7

The Export Directory of Canada
Published by Government Printing Bureau
Author: Canada Department of Trade and Commerce

Techniques of Exporting
Published by Frye Publishing
Author: J R. Arnold
ISBN: 0-919741-56-8

Step by Step Guide To Exporting
Published by Team Canada
Author: Team Canada
ISBN: 066234104X

The Export Marketing Imperative
Published by Thomson
Author: Michael R. Czinkota, Iikka A. Ronkainen, and Maria Ortiz-Bounofina
ISBN: 0-324-22258-0

Multinational Distribution Channel
Tax and Legal Strategies
Author: R. Dudane Hall, Ralph J. Gilbert
ISBN: 0275901157

Successful Cold Call Selling
Published by American Management Association
Author: Lee Boyan
ISBN: 0-8144-7718-6

How To Be Your Own Publicist
Published hill-Hill
Author: Jessica Hatchigan
ISBN:0-07-138332-8

Guerrilla Publicity
Published by Avon, MA: Adams Media Corporation
Author: Jay Conrad Levinson, Rich Frishman and Jill Lublin
ISBN: 1-58062-682-3

Marketing Without Advertising
Author: Michael Phillips, Salli Rasberry
ISBN: 0781726824

The Export Institute of USA
Website: www.exportinstitute.com
Books From the export Institute include:
- The Export Sales and Marketing Manual
  (Often referred to as 'The Bible of Exporting')
- Step-by-Step Analysis of Exporting, locating foreign Markets and Sales Reps, Pricing, Contracts, Shipping and Payment

- 1,200URLS to export websites worldwide
- Foreign Importers and Exporters Sales Leads
- Complete Contact Information on 150,000 Active Import Distributors, Wholesalers and Agents in 137 countries. Data is classified by geographical regions and by the 50,000 types of products they have purchased.
- Become a Successful Export Agent
- Covers basic requirements in education, knowledge, foreign languages, computer skills and finances. Includes errors to avoid and a10 steps action plan.
- International Market Research and Business Intelligence Reports:
  Comprehensive market research studies and industry trade activity reports covering 200 countries, 2,000 categories of products and 16,000 international trading companies.
- Export classroom package for Educators:
  Based upon the export sales and marketing manual, instruction is provided with the most current export information, 100 stimulating topics for classroom discussion and 200 examination question and answers.

Order the above books and publications from the Export Institute of USA by visiting their website: www.exportinstitute.com

Additional sources of Information:

Canada Export Development Corporation
"Road to Exporting: Guide to Federal government Services"
Website: www.infoexport.gc.ca/businesswomen/menu-e.asp

Forum for International Trade Training (FITT)
This body provides training in International Business
Toll Free Phone: 1-800-561-3488
Website: www.fitt.ca

PEMD
Website: www.infoexport.gc.ca

Royal Bank of Canada
Website: www.royalbank.ca

Export Development Corporation
Website: www.edc.ca

Bank of Nova Scotia
Website: www.scotiabank.ca

Team Canada Inc
Toll Free Phone: 1-888-811-1119

Fax: 1-888-449-5444
Website: www.exportsource.gc.ca

Agriculture and Agri-Food Canada
For Canada Agri-Food exporters
Toll Free Phone: 1-888-811-1119
Website: www.ats.agr.ca

Atlantic Canada Opportunities Agency
Website: www.acoa.ca

Canada Economic Development for Quebec Regions
Website: www.dec-ced.gc.ca

Business Development Bank
Toll Free Phone: 1-888-463-6232
Website: www.bdc.ca

British Columbia Trade and Investment Office
Website: www.cse.gov.bc.ca

Win Exports
Website: www.dfait-maneci.gc.ca
Toll Free Phone: 1-800-551-4946

Nova Scotia Export Development Corporation
Website: www.novascotiabusiness.com

Ontario Exports Inc.,
Website: www.ontario-canada.com/export

Marketing/How To Get Business

Hunting for business for your Export/Import firm is about the same as searching for a job in your field. As such, you have to apply all the job search skills you have acquired over the years, customizing them to suit your present need and position.

- Cold calls to manufacturers for information and interviews about who wants to export/import what.
- Make contact with the trade division of Embassies and Consulates of foreign Countries for export/import leads in their countries.
- Visit Chambers of Commerce
- Networking
- Resumes
- Brochure/Flyers
- Business Cards

- Create a Website
- Associations/Social Clubs
- Trade fairs

Good luck!

Chapter 11

INTERNET PHARMACY / MAIL ORDER PHARMACY BUSINESS

Canada has the lowest drug prices of all the developed countries, and with the rising prescription drug prices around the world and in the United States especially, the mail order/internet pharmacy business is actually booming in Canada. For lots of reasons, that may include regulations from the US Federal Government, prescription drug prices are about 50% lower in Canada than in the United States.

As an Internet Pharmacy business owner, you will be providing thousands and millions of patients in the global village with a solution to the rising cost of prescription, non-prescription and over-the –counter medication. You will be offering discount Canadian medication to your clients when they purchase online, by fax, phone and mail, and delivering the medication right to their doorsteps.

You will be doing this task by filling the prescriptions through licensed Canadian Pharmacy/Pharmacies. Therefore, you may not need to stock nor sell any drugs, but rather obtain discount prescription drugs from a licensed Canadian Pharmacy for your clients – a storefront operation.

As an Internet/Online/Mail Order Pharmacy Business owner, you do not necessarily need to be a pharmacist or have any training in the pharmaceutical field.

However, you need:
- A province/state licensed pharmacy
    The licensed Pharmacy will dispense the prescription.
- A Licensed Canadian physician
    The Canadian physician will re-examine the prescription sent by the client to make sure everything is in order. Since all prescription from the customers must be validated by licensed physicians in both the clients country of abode and Canada.
        This means that before your clients receive their medication, it will have been confirmed and handled by at least three professionals- for example: the US physician that prescribed the medication for the US patient, the Canadian physician that examined the prescription, andthe Canadian Pharmacist at the Pharmacy that dispensed the drugs.
        Safe, isn't it?!
- Twenty-four hours call centre attendant/ Customer Service Department

> *The Customer Service will receive and forward the prescription orders as they come in.*

- You must able to accept and process credit card payments
  In this case you need a credit/merchant account or a Paypal account
  Please see the steps for establishing a business online chapter 3 of this book.
- Remember, your clients (clients from the USA) are only allowed, by law to purchase three month's worth of medication for personal use. However, they can order a refill when due.

What You need To Start-Up

- A Computer (with Internet connection)

  Use a desktop or a laptop computer with a 56k modem. Install the following software on the computer:
  - **Word processor (MS Office)** - Use this to write letters, create mailing labels, and address envelopes. In the MS Office you've got MS Word, Excel, Access, Outlook, and PowerPoint.
  - **Spreadsheet** - You can create charts and do your finances 'with a spreadsheet program. Use MS Excel for your spreadsheet needs.
  - **QuickBooks Pro** - With this, you can create custom invoices, compute sales, do electronic banking, pay your bills, control your inventory and payroll. Use it for all accounting and bookkeeping.
  - **Database** - Use a database program to keep records of clients, sellers, vendors and all your business contacts/links. With the database program, you can keep records of phone calls, faxes, meetings, conferences and seminars, and note time and dates of events and incidents. You may want to use MS Access, Dbase or Fox Pro for your database needs.
  - **Graphic** - Use this to create flyers, announcements newsletters and advertisements. You may want to use PageMaker, QuarkXpress and ClarisWorks for your graphic exploits.
  - **Scheduler** - Use this to manage your schedules.
- Phone, Fax, Printer, Scanner, Copier (can buy all-in-one)
- Office Furniture (including office supplies and office accessories)
- Insurance
- Fees payable to become a member in professional and or trade associations.
- Books
- Marketing/advertising cost.
- Business suits, ties, shoes, briefcase (all for personal image improvement) and other miscellaneous expenses

Professional/Trade Associations You May Like To Join/Know:

Canadian International Pharmacy Association
Krys Kirton

Executive Assistant, CIPA
521-70 Arthur Street
Winnipeg, MB Canada R3B 0S5
Telephone: (204) 943-7912
Facsimile: (204) 943-7926
Website: www.ciparx.ca
E-mail: krys.kirton@ciparx.ca

International Pharmacy Association of British Columbia
www.ipabc.ca
Email: contact@ipabc.ca
Manitoba International Pharmacists Association
PO Box 40068
1131 Nairn Ave. Manitoba
R2L 2G2
www.mipa.ca
info@mipa.ca

Internet and Mail Order Pharmacy Accreditation Commission – IMPAC Inc.
P.O. Box 1146
Manchester, Vermont 05254
USA FAX: 1-413-443-9724
1-800-677-7019
1-413-443-9780
www.impacsurvey.org

Alberta College of Pharmacists
Gregory E. Eberhart
Registrar
10303 Jasper Ave, Suite 1200
Edmonton, Alberta
T5J 3N6 Canada
Phone: 780/990-0321
Fax: 780/990-0328
Web site: http://www.pharmacists.ab.ca/college/default.aspx
E-mail: greg.eberhart@pharmacists.ab.ca

College of Pharmacists of British Columbia
Marshall Moleschi
Registrar
200 - 1765 W 8th Ave
Vancouver, British Columbia
V6J 1V8 Canada
Phone: 604/733-2440
Fax: 604/733-2493
Web site: www.bcpharmacists.org

E-mail: marshall.moleschi@bcpharmacists.org

Manitoba Pharmaceutical Association
Ronald F. Guse
Registrar
187 Saint Mary's Rd
Winnipeg, Manitoba
R2H 1J2 Canada
Phone: 204/233-1411
Fax: 204/237-3468
Web site: www.mpha.mb.ca
E-mail: marshall.moleschi@bcpharmacists.org
info@mpha.mb.ca

New Brunswick Pharmaceutical Society
Bill Veniot
Registrar
373 Urquhart Ave, Unit B
Moncton, New Brunswick
E1H 2R4 Canada
Phone: 506/857-8957
Fax: 506/857-8838
Web site: www.napra.org
E-mail: bill.veniot@nbpharmacists.ca

Nova Scotia College of Pharmacists
Susan Wedlake
Registrar
1526 Dresden Row 7th Floor
Halifax: , Nova Scotia
B3J 3K3 Canada
Phone: 902/422-8528
Fax: 902/422-0885
Web site: www.napra.ca
E-mail: s.wedlake@ns.sympatico.ca

Ontario College of Pharmacists
Deanna L. Williams
Registrar
483 Huron St
Toronto, ON
M5R 2R4 Canada
Phone: 416/962-4861
Fax: 416/847-8200
Web site: www.ocpinfo.com
E-mail: dwilliams@ocpinfo.com

Prince Edward Island Pharmacy Board
Neila I. Auld
Registrar
PO Box 89, Unit 7 – 20424 TCH
Crapaud, PE
C0A 1J0 Canada
Phone: 902/658-2780
Fax: 902/658-2198
Web site: www.napra.org
E-mail: peipharm@pei.aibn.com

Quebec Order of Pharmacists
Pierre Ducharme
Registrar
266, Rue Notre-Dame Ouest
Bureau 301
Montreal, QC
H2Y 1T6 Canada
Phone: 514/284-9588
Fax: 514/284-3420
Web site: www.opq.org
E-mail: ordrepharm@opq.org

Pharmacy Examining Board of Canada (PEBC)
John Pugsley
Registrar/Treasurer
415 Yonge St, Suite 601
Toronto, ON
M5B 2E7 Canada
Phone: 416/979-2431
Fax: 416/599-9244
Web site: www.pebc.ca
E-mail: marshall.moleschi@bcpharmacists.org
pebccdn@attglobal.net

National Association of Pharmacy Regulatory Authorities (NAPRA)
Kenneth A. Potvin
Executive Director
220 Laurier Ave W, Suite 750
Ottawa, ON
K1P 5Z9 Canada
Phone: 613/569-9658
Fax: 613/569-9659
Web site: www.napra.org
E-mail: info@napra.ca or kpotvin@napra.ca

Other Useful Resources – International Pharmacy Links:

Canadian Pharmaceutical Association
http://www.cdnpharm.ca/
Canadian Society for Pharmaceutical Sciences (CSPS)
http://www.ualberta.ca/~csps/
http://www.ualberta.ca/
International Academy of Compounding Pharmacists (IACP)
http://www.iacprx.org/
International Pharmaceutical Federation (FIP)
http://www.fip.nl/
Pharmacy Guild of Australia
http://www.guild.org.au/
List of international societies
http://www.pharmweb.net/pwmirror/

Books You May Need To Buy:

Most of the books you may need are the books on steps to establishing a business online, internet marketing and marketing in general.

The Unofficial Guide to Starting a Business Online
Published by Wiley Publishing, Inc.
Author: Jason R. Rich
ISBN0-02-863340-7

Doing Big Business on the Internet
Published by Self-Counsel Press
Author: Hurley & Birkwood
ISBN: 1-55180-119-1

Selling On The Web
Author: Paul Galloway
ISBN: 1563824876
Start an eBay Business

Published by Alpha Books
Author: Barbara Weltman
ISBN: 159257-333-9

Small Business Online: A Strategic Guide for Canada Entrepreneurs
Published by Prentice Hall Canada Inc.,
Author: Jim Carroll with Rich Broadhead
ISBN: 0-13-976895-5

101 Ways To Promote your Website
Published by Maximum Press
Author: Susan Sweeney
ISBN: 1931644217

Start Your Own Business On eBay: Your Step by Step Guide To Success
Published by Entrepreneur Press
Author: Jacquelyn Lynn
ISBN: 1932531122

Start Your Own E-Business
Published by Entrepreneur Press
Author: Entrepreneur Press
ISBN: 1932156747

Selling On The Net: The Complete Guide
Published by NTC Business Books
Author: Lewis, Herschell Gordon
ISBN: 0844232343

Selling On The Internet: How To Open An Electronic Storefront And Have Millions Of Customers Come To You
Published by McGraw-Hill
Author: James C. Gonyea, Wayne M. Gonyea
ISBN: 0070241872

The Online Business Book
Published by Adam Media Corporation
Author: Rob Liflander
ISBN: 158062-3204

Guerrilla Marketing Online
Published by Houghton Mifflin
Author: Jay Conrad Levinson and Charles Rubin
ISBN: 0-395-86061-X

Internet Marketing For Dummies
Published by Wiley Publishing Inc.,
ISBN: 0-7645-0778-8

Low-Cost Website Promotion
Published by Adam Media Corporation
Author: Barry Feig
ISBN: 1-58062-501-0

Online Business Resources
Published by Made E-Z
Author: Paul Galloway
ISBN: 1-56382-510-4

Generating Trust in Online Business: From Theory To Practice
Published by IQ
Author: Magda Fusaro
ISBN: 2-922417-28-X

Absolute Beginners Guide To Launching an eBay Business
Published by Que
Author: Michael Miller
ISBN: 0-7897-3058-8

Starting an eBay Business For Dummies
Published by Wiley Publishing Inc.,
Author: Marsha Collier
ISBN: 0-7645-6924-4

Online Business Planning
Published by Career Press
Author: Robert T. Gorman
ISBN: 1-56414-369-4

Guerrilla Publicity
Published by Adams Media Corporation
Author: Jay Conrad Levinson, Rich Frishman, Jill Lublin
ISBN: 1-58062-682-3

Marketing Without Advertising
Author: Michael Phillips, Salli Rasberry
ISBN: 0873376080

The 22 Immutable Laws of Marketing
Published by Harper Business
Author: Al Ries and Jack Trout
ISBN: 0887306667

6 Steps To Free Publicity
Published by Career Press Inc
Author: Marcia Yudkin
ISBN: 1-56414-675-8

Endless Referrals: Network Your Everyday Contacts into Sales (New and Updated Edition)
Author: Bob Burg
ISBN: 0070089973

Marketing/How to get business
- Promote your website to increase the number of visitors.
- Advertise in the Yellow Pages, newspapers, magazines, and billboards
- Create brochures and flyers
- Business cards

Good luck!

Chapter 12

MAGAZINE PUBLISHING

Going into the business of magazine publishing has never been easier than it is today. However, going into the business of magazine publishing is not really what matters the most - staying in business is the most difficult part of magazine publishing. It is also important to know that magazine publishing is not, at best, a one-man business.

To start a magazine publishing business, you need to have a cause- have something to say and be able to live and say it in the long haul. Be sure the subject of your publication is something you know very well. You need to identify the audience for your subject, and find out what they really want to read and see in your publication. Use this to create the publisher-reader bond that will sustain your publishing business and bring you financial success. Study and learn as much as possible about publishing, and obtain help and advice from experienced people in the field of publishing before going into the business.

Before starting a magazine publishing business, ask yourself, and answer the following questions:
- What will the content of my magazine be?
- How do I organize staff or contributors?
- Who is my audience?
- Is the market large enough to sustain my magazine in the long run?
- Will I be able to convert the casual readers of the magazine into regular readers?
- What will be the scale of my publication?
- Who will be my printer?
- What will my design and layout look like?
- How much will it cost me to start up?
- How will I get advertisers?
- How will I get subscribers for the magazine?
- How much will I charge for the subscription?
- How do I go about distribution?
- Will I be able to get the magazine on the newsstands?
- How long will it take for me to start generating revenue?

After answering the questions, you will be able to make a decision on the type and branch of magazine publishing you will be embarking on, Such as: Literary, science, fashion, business, beauty, environmental, music, education, automotive, computer topics, aircraft, pictorial, consumer products, food products, food recipes, etc. No matter type of magazine you choose to publish, you will need the following:

What You need To Start-Up

- A Computer (with Internet connection)

  Use a desktop or a laptop computer with a 56k modem. Install the following software and hardware on the computer:
  - o **Word processor (MS Office) -** Use this to write letters, create mailing labels, and address envelopes. In the MS Office you've got MS Word, Excel, Access, Outlook, and PowerPoint.
  - o **Spreadsheet** - You can create charts and do your finances with a spreadsheet program. Use MS Excel for your spreadsheet needs.
  - o **QuickBooks Pro** - With this, you can create custom invoices, compute sales, do electronic banking, pay your bills, control your inventory and payroll. Use it for all accounting and bookkeeping.
  - o **Database** - Use a database program to keep records of clients, sellers, vendors and all your business contacts/links. With the database program, you can keep records of phone calls, faxes, meetings, conferences and seminars, and note time and dates of events and incidents. You may want to use MS Access, Dbase or Fox Pro for your database needs.
  - o **Graphic** - Use this to create flyers, announcements newsletters and advertisements. You may want to use PageMaker, QuarkXpress and ClarisWorks for your graphic exploits.
  - o **Scheduler** - Use this to manage your schedules.
  - o **Magazine publishing Software**
  - o **A Zip drive or CD-R (CD-ROM Recordable)**
  - o **FTP software**
  - o **Scribus: www.scribus.org.uk**
    This is an open-source page layout program. It is available for Linux
  - o **The GIMP: www.gimp.org**
    It is a GPL photo-editing program. It is available from Linux, OS X and Windows.
  - o **Inkscape: www.inkscape.org**
    It is an open-source vector graphics program for Linux and OS X
- Web Hosting
- A good digital camera
- Phone, Fax, Printer, Scanner, Copier (can buy all-in-one)
- Office Furniture (including office supplies and office accessories)
- Insurance
- Fees payable to become a member in professional and or trade associations.
- Books

- Marketing/advertising cost.
- Business suits, ties, shoes, briefcase (all for personal image improvement) and other miscellaneous expenses

Professional/Trade Associations You May Like To Join/Know:

The Council of Literary Magazines and Presses
154 Christopher Street, Suite 3C
New York, NY 10014-9110
Phone: (212) 741-9110
Fax: (212) 741-9112
Website: www.clmp.org
For general inquiries: info@clmp.org

Canadian Magazine Publishers Association
Phone: 416-504-0274 ext 221
Fax: 416-504-0437
Website: www.cmpa.ca
Email: info@cmpa.ca

British Columbia Association of Magazine Publishers
Phone: 604-688-1175

The Periodical Writers Association of Canada
Phone: 416-504-1645
Website: www.pwac.ca
Email: info@pwac.ca
Canada's National Poetry Magazine
Website: www.arcpoetry.ca
Email: arc@arcpoetry.ca

BC Association of Magazine Publishers
Phone: 604-688-1175
Fax: 604-687-1274
Website: www.bcamp.bc.ca
Email: info@bcamp.bc.ca

The Canada Council for the Arts
Phone: 1-800-263-5588
Fax: 613-566-439
TTY: 613-565-5194
Website: www.canadacouncil.ca
Email: info@canadacouncil.ca

The Canadian Bookbinders and Book Artists Guild
Shelagh Smith, Managing Director

Phone: 416-581-1071
Fax: 416-581-1053
Website: www.cbbag.ca
Email: cbbag@web.net

Canadian Booksellers Association
Toll-free: 1-866-788-0790
Phone: 416-467-7883
Fax: 416-467-7886
Website: www.cbabook.org
Email: sdayus@cbabook.org

Ontario Community Newspapers Association
3050 Harvester Rd., Suite 103
Burlington, Ontario
L7N 3J1
Tel: 905-639-8720
Fax: 905-639-6962
Web site: www.ocna.org

British Columbia and Yukon Community Newspaper association
122-1020 Mainland Street
Vancouver, B.C. V6B 2T4
Canada
Tel: 604-669-9222
Toll-free: 1-866-669-9222
Fax: 604-684-4713
Website: www.bccommunitynews.com
Email: info@bccommunitynews.com

Atlantic Community Newspapers Association
2 Bluewater Road, Suite 205
Bedford, Nova Scotia, B4B 1G7
Toll-free: 1.877.842.4480
Fax: (902) 832.4484
Website: www.acna.com

Alberta Weekly Newspapers Association
Suite 800
4445 Calgary Trail South
Edmonton, AB
T6H 5R7
Phone: 800-282-6903
780-434-8746
Fax: 780- 438-8356
Website: www.awna.ab.ca

E-mail: info@awna.com

Canadian Business Press
4195 Dundas Street West
Suite 346
Toronto, Ontario
M8X 1Y4
Phone: 416-239-1022
Fax: 416-239-1076
Website: www.cbp.ca
Email: admin@cbp.ca

The Canadian Association of Journalists
Algonquin College
1385 Woodroffe Avenue, B224
Ottawa, Ontario
K2G 1V8
Telephone 613-526-8061
Fax: 613-521-3904
Email: caj@igs.net

Canadian Community Newspapers Association
8 Market Street, Suite 300
Toronto, Ontario
M5E 1M6
1-877-305-2262
Website: www.ccna.ca
Email: info@ccna.ca

Magazine Publishers of America
810 Seventh Avenue, 24th Floor
between 52nd and 53rd streets
New York, NY 10019
Phone: 212-872-3700
Website: www.magazine.org
Email: mpa@magazine.org

Small Publishers Association of North America
1618 West Colorado Avenue
Colorado Springs, CO, 80904
Please Call: 719-475-1726
Fax: 719-471-2182
Website: www.spanet.org
Email: span@spannet.org

The Canadian Publishers' Council
250 Merton Street, Suite 203,
Toronto, Ontario
M4S 1B1.
Phone: 416-322-7011
Fax :416-322-6999.
Website: www.pubcouncil.ca

Literary Press Group of Canada (LPG)
192 Spadina Avenue, Suite 501
Toronto, Ontario
M5T 2C2
Phone: 416-483-1321
Fax: 416-483-2510
Website: www.ipg.ca
Email: info@ipg.ca

Books You May Need To Buy:

Launch Your Own Magazine: A Guide For Succeeding in Today's Marketplace
By Samir Husni,
Website: www.mrmagazine.com

The Magazine: Everything You Need to Know to Make It in the Magazine Business
By Leonard Mogel
Website: www.magazine.org

Starting and Running a Successful Newsletter or Magazine
By Cheryl Woodard
Published by Nolo Press

How to start and Produce a Magazine or Newsletter
By Gordon Woolf

How to Make Newsletters and Magazines that Will Last
By Cheryl Woodard

How to Start a Magazine
By James Kobak

Publish Your Own Magazine or Weekly Newspaper
By Thomas A. Williams

The Magazine: From Cover to Cover.
NTC Publishing Group,
By Johnson, Sammye and Prijatel Patricia.

Career Opportunities in Magazine Publishing.
Monti Ralph

Magazine Career Directory
Morgan, Bradley
By Visible Ink Press

Other Resources/Useful Links:

The Magazine Publishers of America
Website: www.magazine.org

www.publishingbiz.com

www.magazinepublisher.com

Marketing/How To Get Business

Hunting for business for your Magazine is about the same thing as searching for a job in your field. As such, you have to apply all the job search skills you have acquired over the years, customizing them to suit your present need and position.
- Cold calls to Companies, Businesses, Schools, Organizations and Events/ Conference/Convention Organizers for information and interviews about who may need to advertise in the pages of your magazine.
- Find out and incorporate the marketing methods and approaches of other professionals in your field into your own method and approach
- Network with other professionals and everybody at any opportunity
- Yellow Pages advertisement
- Brochure/Flyers
- Business Cards
- Create a Website
- Associations/Social Clubs
- Distribute gift certificates and discounted subscription packages to clients to give to their friends
- Send out Advertising/subscription package offers for special days and seasons
- Keep in touch with your clients and call the clients who have discontinued subscription for some time to remind them of your good services and new offer new discounted offers that are available
- Call your clients - new/old and regulars, weeks, months and or years after they use your services to thank them for using the services of your Magazine, but above all, to ask them how they are doing and how satisfied they are with the result of the earlier ad campaign.
- Offer free advertising/subscription packages to your regular clients for referrals - if they bring in four or more new clients

- Speak to business owners - most business owners like to have new papers/ magazines in their shops/offices
- Use the services of sales people and street hawkers
- Get your Magazine to the newsstands
- Create a free distribution model
- Check residential and business high-rise management for daily/weekly supply
- Strive to establish a good and comfortable relationship with readers
- Add ancillary products and services, such as spin-off publications, trade shows etc.
- Constantly develop a product that is responsive to the needs of your subscribers, advertisers and casual readers.
- Get influential people to share their thoughts in your magazine

Good luck!

Chapter 13

MANUFACTURER'S / INDEPENDENT SALES REPRESENTATIVE

Manufacturer's/sales representatives are paid commissions on sales of goods/ services they make for manufacturers/service companies. Such sales may be realised nationally and or internationally. A manufacturer's/sales representative may choose to deal in a particular industry or line of product. The products may range from raw material through semi-finished to finished products, and services may range from repair through maintenance to entertainment, education and health services. The sales may be to retailers, wholesalers, or a manufacturer or from one service provider to another.

A manufacturer's /Independent Sales Representative has a duty to:

- Employ the best of efforts to sell and promote the product/services of the company/industry he/she is representing
- Meet sales quota requirements
- Represent the product/services at trade fairs and trade shows
- Be able to report and forecast sales within a reasonable margin of error
- Have and maintain a comprehensive list of clients
- The responsibility to protect intellectual and or industrial property rights
- Respond to all sales inquiries

As a Manufacturer's/Independent Sales Representative, you need:

- To be people smart
- Possess charm - being accessible, listening to people, addressing people by their names, being generally warm, good appearance and knowing how to talk to people, and how to explain things to people, are extremely important when selling, and are invariably required to be a good salesperson.
- Good Knowledge of the product/services you are selling
- A chemist selling chemical reagents and laboratory equipment must already have good background knowledge of the product he/she is selling. Having the knowledge of the products /services you are selling makes it easier for you as a salesperson.
- Some manufacturer's/sales representatives represent a number of companies

and or products round the globe. If you want to work in that capacity then you will need to learn foreign languages and cultures.

What You need To Start-Up

- A Computer (with Internet connection)

  Use a desktop or a laptop computer with a 56k modem. Install the following software on the computer:
  - **Word processor (MS Office)** - Use this to write letters, create mailing labels, and address envelopes. In the MS Office you've got MS Word, Excel, Access, Outlook, and PowerPoint.
  - **Spreadsheet** - You can create charts and do your finances with a spreadsheet program. Use MS Excel for your spreadsheet needs.
  - **QuickBooks Pro** - With this, you can create custom invoices, compute sales, do electronic banking, pay your bills, control your inventory and payroll. Use it for all accounting and bookkeeping.
  - **Database** - Use a database program to keep records of clients, sellers, vendors and all your business contacts/links. With the database program, you can keep records of phone calls, faxes, meetings, conferences and seminars, and note time and dates of events and incidents. You may want to use MS Access, Dbase or Fox Pro for your database needs.
  - **Graphic** - Use this to create flyers, announcements newsletters and advertisements. You may want to use PageMaker, QuarkXpress and ClarisWorks for your graphic exploits.
  - **Scheduler** - Use this to manage your schedules.
  - **The following software are specially designed for you, the Manufacturer's/Independent Sales Representative**
    - Representative Profit Management System (RPMS) Website: www.rpms.com
    - Manufacturers Agents Computer System (MACS) Website; www.macsworld.com
    - WinRep Software Website: www.winrep.com
    - Reps for Windows Website: www.repworld.com
- Phone, Fax, Printer, Scanner, Copier (can buy all-in-one)
- Office Furniture (including office supplies and office accessories)
- Insurance
- Fees payable to become a member in professional and or trade associations.
- Books
- Marketing/advertising cost.
- Business suits, ties, shoes, briefcase (all for personal image improvement) and other miscellaneous expenses

The total cost of your start-up needs will not exceed $20,000 Canadian.

Professional/Trade Associations You May Like To Join/Know:

Canadian Association of Manufacturers Representatives

Canadian Association of Independent Sales representatives

The Alliance of Manufacturer's and Exporters Canada
1 Nicholas Street,
Suite 1500
Ottawa, Ontario
K1N 7B7
Phone: 613-238-8888
Website: www.the-alliance.org

5995 Avesbury Road
Suite 900
Mississauga, Ontario
L5R 3P9
Phone: 905-568-8300

75 International Boulevard,
Suite 400
Toronto, On
M9W 6L9
Phone: 416-798-8000
Fax: 416-798-8050

Automotive Parts Manufacturers Association
195 The West Mall, Suite 516
Toronto, Ontario
M9C 5K1
Phone: 416-620-4220
Fax: 417-620-9730
Website: www.apma@interware.net

Canadian Chemical Producers Association
Phone: 1-800-267-6666
Fax: 613-237-40-61

Canadian Sanitation Supply Association
300 Mill Road, Suite G-10
Etobicoke, Ontario
M9C 4W7
Phone: 416-620-9320

Fax: 416-620-7199
Email: info@cssa.com

Machinery and Equipment Manufacturers Association of Canada
116 Albert Street, Suite 701
Ottawa, Ontario
K1P 5G3
Phone: 613-232-7213

Canadian Plastic Industry Association
5925 Airport Road, Suite 500
Mississauga, Ontario
L4V 1W1
Phone: 905-678-7748
Fax: 905-678-0774

Non-prescription Drug Manufacturers Association of Canada
1111 Prince of Wales Drive, Suite 406
Ottawa, Ontario
K2C 3T2
Phone: 613-723-0777
Fax: 613-723-0779
Email: ndmac@ndmac.ca

Automotive Industries Association of Canada
1272 Wellington Street
Ottawa, Ontario
K1Y 3A7
Phone: 613-728-5821
Fax: 613-728-6021
Email: aia@aiacanada.com
Website: www.aftmkt.com/associations

Aerospace Industries Association of Canada
60 Queen Street, Suite 1200
Ottawa, Ontario
K1P 5Y7
Phone: 613-232-4297
Fax: 613-232-1142
Website: www.aiac.ca

Canadian Association of Mining Equipment and Services for Export
345 Renfrew Drive, Suite 101
Markham, Ontario
L3R 9S9
Phone: 1-905-513-1834

Email: minesupply@camese.org

North American Industries Representatives Association (NIRA)
Website: www.nira.org
Ontario Motor Vehicle Industry Council
36 York Mills Road, Suite 110
North York, Ontario
M2P 2E9
Phone: 416-226-4500
Toll Free: 1-800-943-6002
Website: www.omvic.on.ca

Books You May Need To Buy:

Selling Through Independent Representatives
Published by AMACON
Author: Harold J. Novick
ISBN: 0-8144-0522-3
Thomas Register of Manufacturers
Website: www.thomasregister.com

The Export Directory of Canada
Contains a List of Canadian Manufacturers, Procedures and Exports

A list of Manufacturing Firms in British Columbia
Segregated by size, groups according to employment
Published by Victoria British Columbia
Author: BC Bureau of Economics and Statistics

Your Guide to Statistics Canada's New Census of Manufacturers Publication

Selling to Government
A Guide to Government Procurement in Canada
Multinational Distribution Channel

Tax and legal strategies
Author: R. Dudane Hall, Ralph J. Gilbert
ISBN: 0275901157

Successful Cold Call Selling
Published by American Management Association
Author: Lee Boyan
ISBN: 0-8144-7718-6

How To Be Your Own Publicist
Published Hill-Hill

Author: Jessica Hatchigan
ISBN:0-07-138332-8

Guerrilla Publicity
Published by Adams Media Corporation
Author: Jay Conrad Levinson, Rich Frishman and Jill Lublin
ISBN: 1-58062-682-3

Marketing without Advertising
Author: Michael Phillips, Salli Rasberry
ISBN: 0873376080

Other Sources of Information:

The Canadian chamber of Commerce
BCE Place
181 Bay Street
P.O.BOX 818
Toronto, Ontario
M5J 2T3
Phone: 416-868-6415
Fax: 416-868-0189
Website: www.chamber.ca

Ontario Chamber of Commerce
2345 Yonge Street, Suite 808
Toronto, Ontario
M4P 2E5
Phone: 416-482-5222
Website: www.occ.on.ca

- Chambers of Commerce may provide lists of Manufacturers, Service Firms and Government Agencies
- Trade fairs
- You may also want to have a look at the books and sources of information for the Export/Import Agent.

Marketing/How To Get Business

Hunting for business for your Manufacturer's/Independent sales Reps firm is about the same as searching for a job/contract in your field. As such, you have to apply all the job search skills you have learnt over the years, customizing them to suit your present need and position.
- Cold calls to manufacturers/Service industries for information and interviews about who wants the services of a Sales Representative.

- Make contact with the trade division of Embassies and Consulates of foreign Countries for Representation leads in their countries.
- Visit Chambers of Commerce
- Resumes
- Brochure/Flyers
- Business Cards
- Create a Website
- Join Associations/Social Clubs
- Trade Fairs

Good luck!

Chapter 14

MARKETING/ADVERTISING AGENCY

As an Advertising/Marketing Agent, your agency will be employing attractive packages, designs and or appealing information to bring products and or services to the attention of the public, with the sole purpose of getting the public to buy the products or use the services.

The marketing/advertising agency reaches the audience through:
- Television
- Radio
- The internet
- Newspapers
- Magazines
- Seminars
- Conferences
- Door-to-Door

The Agency may choose to specialize in a particular industry, product or line of products, and or services.

The agency may also choose to market/advertise using a specific channel: Television, Radio, Online, Newspapers, Magazines, Seminars, Conferences, or Door-to-Door.

It is advisable that your agency markets/advertises for the industry, products, and services related to your profession, where you already know the literature, trends, approaches and the location and times of conferences and seminars.

As a marketing/advertising agent, you need:
- To understand marketing/advertising as an industry/trade
- Knowledge of the products/services you are advertising
- Knowledge of how to use your chosen medium effectively

What You need To Start-Up

- A Computer (with Internet connection)
  Use a desktop or a laptop computer with a 56k modem. Install the following

software on the computer:

- o **Word processor (MS Office) -** Use this to write letters, create mailing labels, and address envelopes. In the MS Office you've got MS Word, Excel, Access, Outlook, and PowerPoint.
- o **Spreadsheet** - You can create charts and do your finances with a spreadsheet program. Use MS Excel for your spreadsheet needs.
- o **QuickBooks Pro** - With this, you can create custom invoices, compute sales, do electronic banking, pay your bills, control your inventory and payroll. Use it for all accounting and bookkeeping.
- o **Database** - Use a database program to keep records of clients, sellers, vendors and all your business contacts/links. With the database program, you can keep records of phone calls, faxes, meetings, conferences and seminars, and note time and dates of events and incidents. You may want to use MS Access, Dbase or Fox Pro for your database needs.
- o **Graphic** - Use this to create flyers, announcements newsletters and advertisements. You may want to use PageMaker, QuarkXpress and ClarisWorks for your graphic exploits.
- o **Scheduler** - Use this to manage your schedules.
- Phone, Fax, Printer, Scanner, Copier (can buy all-in-one)
- Office Furniture (including office supplies and office accessories)
- Insurance
- Fees payable to become a member in professional and or trade associations.
- Books
- Marketing/advertising cost.
- Business suits, ties, shoes, briefcase (all for personal image improvement) and other miscellaneous expenses

The total cost of your start-up needs will not exceed $20,000 Canadian.

Books You May Need To Buy:

How to Open and Run a Home-Based Communication Business
Published by Globe Pequot Press
Author: Louann Nagy and Werksman
ISBN: 1564406318

The 22 Irrefutable Laws of Advertising and When to Violate Them
Published by John Wiley & Sons Asia Pte Ltd.
Author: Micheal Newman
ISBN: 0470-82106-X

The 22 Immutable Laws of Marketing
Published by Harper Business
Author: Al Ries and Jack Trout
ISBN: 0887306667

How To Start And Run Your Own Advertising Agency
Published by McGraw-Hill
Author: Allan Krieff
ISBN: 0070352194

6 Steps To Free Publicity
Published by Career Press Inc.
Author: Marcia Yudkin
ISBN: 1-56414-675-8

Public Relations: Strategies And Tactics
Published by Addison Wesley Publishing
Author: Dennis L. Wilcox
ISBN: 0321015479

The Practice of Public Relations
Published by Princetice Hall
Author: Fraser Seitel
ISBN: 0131020250

Guerrilla Publicity
Published by Adams Media Corporation
Author: Jay Conrad Levinson, Rich Frishman and Jill Lublin
ISBN: 1-58062-682-3

How To Be Your Own Publicist
Published by McGraw-Hill
Author: Jessica Hatchigan
ISBN:0-07-138332-8

Marketing Without Advertising
Author: Michael Phillips, Salli Rasberry
ISBN: 0873376080

Marketing/How To Get Business

Hunting for business for your Marketing/Advertising Agency is about the same thing as searching for job/contract in your field. As such, you have to apply all the job search skills you have acquired over the years, customizing them to suit your present need and position.
Cold calls to Companies and Businesses for information and interviews about who may need the services, and provide them with reasons why they may need the services of your agency.
- Networking
- Resumes

- Brochure/Flyers
- Business Cards
- Create a Website
- Join Associations/social clubs
- Trade fairs

Good luck!

Chapter 15

MAINTENANCE AND REPAIR SERVICES

There are vast number of things that require maintenance and repair, including:
- Computers (including monitors and printers)
- Small engines
- Medical equipment
- Hospital equipment
- Dental equipment
- Laboratory equipment
- Engineering equipment

And other less sophisticated things like: Watches, Clocks, Televisions, VCRs, DVD Players, Fax Machines, Scanners, Copiers, CD Players, Fridges, Radios, Coffee machines, Expresso machines, Cash register machines, Lawn mowers, Projectors, Vacuum cleaners, Telephones, Home/Kitchen appliances, Hair dryers, etc.

Some of the maintenance and repair services require:
- Training
- Certification
- License
- To be in the business of Maintenance and Repair services, you need:
- Technical aptitude
- Certification, where necessary
- Training
- Licenses, where necessary
- A Vehicle (in some cases)
- Replacement parts

What You Need to Start-Up

- A Computer (with Internet connection)

   Use a desktop or a laptop computer with a 56k modem. Install the following software on the computer:
   - **Word processor (MS Office) -** Use this to write letters, create mailing

labels, and address envelopes. In the MS Office you've got MS Word, Excel, Access, Outlook, and PowerPoint.

o **Spreadsheet** - You can create charts and do your finances with a spreadsheet program. Use MS Excel for your spreadsheet needs.

o **QuickBooks Pro** - With this, you can create custom invoices, compute sales, do electronic banking, pay your bills, control your inventory and payroll. Use it for all accounting and bookkeeping.

o **Database** - Use a database program to keep records of clients, sellers, vendors and all your business contacts/links. With the database program, you can keep records of phone calls, faxes, meetings, conferences and seminars, and note time and dates of events and incidents. You may want to use MS Access, Dbase or Fox Pro for your database needs.

o **Graphic** - Use this to create flyers, announcements newsletters and advertisements. You may want to use PageMaker, QuarkXpress and ClarisWorks for your graphic exploits.

o **Scheduler** - Use this to manage your schedules.

o **The following software are specially designed for you, the Manufacturer's/Independent Sales Representative**
  - Representative Profit Management System (RPMS)
    Website: www.rpms.com
  - Manufacturers Agents Computer System (MACS)
    Website; www.macsworld.com
  - WinRep Software
    Website: www.winrep.com
  - Reps for Windows
    Website: www.repworld.com

- Phone, Fax, Printer, Scanner, Copier (can buy all-in-one)
- Office Furniture (including office supplies and office accessories)
- Digital photo camera
- Insurance
- Fees payable to become a member in professional and or trade associations.
- Books
- Marketing/advertising cost.

The total cost of your start-up needs will not exceed $20,000 Canadian.

Books You May Need To Buy:

Start Your Own Computer Repair Business
Published by McGraw-Hill
Author: Linda Rohrbough, Michael F. Hordeski
ISBN: 0079119018

The Computer and Network Professional's Certification Guide
Published by Sybex publishing

Author: J Scott Christianson with Lee Fajen
ISBN: 0782122604
Website: www.certification-upgrade.com

How To Start Your Own Appliance Repair Business from Home Without Capital or Experience: For Major Appliances
Author: Loughurst Rey D
ISBN: 1563021102

Opportunities in Installation and Repair Careers
Published by VGM Career Horizons
Author: Mark Rowh
ISBN: 0844241369

How to Start and Manage a Farm Equipment Repair Service Business
ISBN: 1887005269

Upgrading and Repairing PC's Quick Reference
Author: Scott Mueller
ISBN: 0789716690

Marketing Without Advertising
Author: Michael Phillips, Salli Rasberry
ISBN: 0873376080

Guerrilla Publicity
Published by Adams Media Corporation
Author: Jay Conrad Levinson, Rich Frishman, Jill Lublin
ISBN: 1-58062-682-3

Marketing/How To Get Business

Hunting for business for your Maintenance and Repair firm is about the same as searching for a job/contract in your field. As such, you have to apply all the job search skills you have learnt over the years, customizing them to suit your present need and position.

- Cold calls to companies and businesses for information and interviews about who may need the services, and to provide them with reasons they may need the maintenance and repair services of your Firm.
- Networking
- Yellow pages advertisement
- Brochure/Flyers
- Business Cards
- Create a Website
- Join Associations/social clubs

- Trade Fairs

Good luck!

Chapter 16

MEDICAL/HEALTH TOURISM BUSINESS

Travelling to other countries, especially to developing nations for the purposes of elective medical procedure, cosmetic surgery, dental surgery, plastic surgery, in-vitro fertilization, male and female fertility treatments, or eye surgery in combination with wellness, leisure and relaxation directed to reinvigorating an individual's physical, mental and emotional state is what is today termed medical tourism. This multi-billion dollar industry is booming more than ever before.

As a medical tourism business owner, you will be out-sourcing medical treatment and services for a far lower price plus sightseeing and more, to developing countries to be performed primarily by Canadian, American, and British trained specialists.

On the other hand, wealthy individuals from developing countries who desire some "brand name surgery", come to Canada or the United States to undergo either life-threatening surgery or cosmetic medical procedures. No matter which way the tide goes, you, as a medical tourism firm, are in business.

In some cases, patients travel to developing countries from North America to undergo life-threatening surgeries.

Reasons people indulge in medical/health tourism vary depending on the individual, and they may include:
- Less expensive – a fraction of what it costs in the western nations, sometimes 1/10th – 1/20th
- Long waiting times for surgeries in developed nations – sometimes for years
- Procedures not covered by basic insurance

In Canada you may qualify for reimbursement for out-of-country medical treatment if you meet the criteria. The criteria may differ from province to province.

In Ontario - OHIP
Ontario Ministry of Health and Long-Term Care
Payment for out-of-country health services with prior approval

OHIP may pay full cost for health services outside Canada if:
- The patient obtained a written authorization from the Ministry of Health and

Long-Term Care before the treatment was administered
- The treatment is generally accepted in Ontario
- The treatment or an equivalent procedure is not available or performed in Ontario
- The treatment is available in Ontario but there was a necessity that the person travel outside Canada to avoid a delay that may have resulted in death or medically significant, irreversible damage.

In order to qualify for full funding of treatment performed outside Canada, your Ontario physician must apply to the Ministry of Health and Long-Term Care for approval while you are still in Ontario, before you travel and undergo an out-of-country treatment.

For more Information, call:

Ministry information line at 1-800-268-1154
(Toll-free in Ontario only)
In Toronto, call 416-314-5518
TTY 1-800-387-5559

In British Columbia
Ministry of Health Services, Government of British Columbia

Referring a Patient for Medical Services Outside of Canada:
- Prior authorization from the Ministry of Health Services is required for payment for services rendered outside of Canada.
- The presiding medical specialist needs to submit either a written request for approval.
- The approval by the ministry depends on the following criteria:
- The procedure would be a benefit if performed in British Columbia
- The treatment will be performed by a licensed physician
- The procedure is medically required
- The procedure needs to be performed outside Canada
- The treatment is generally accepted in British Columbia
- The treatment or an equivalent procedure is not available or performed in Canada
- Delay in accessing treatment may result in medically significant consequences for the patient
- The service is provided in an accredited hospital.

For more information contact:
1 866 456 6950
Medical Services Plan
PO Box 9480
Stn Prov Govt
Victoria, B.C. V8W 9E7
Phone: 250 952-2668
Vancouver: 604 456 6950

Other provinces in Canada have the same process. The only difference is that the patient will pay up-front and get the refund later from the ministry of health.

Countries that are actively involved in promoting medical tourism include:
- South Africa
- India
- Thailand
- Cuba
- Malaysia
- Venezuela
- The Philipines
- Costa Rica
- Singapore

.....with many more countries shaping services aimed at medical tourism.

South Africa

Medical tourism in South Africa encourages safari-visits, stays in luxurious hotels, picturesque mountain and seaside resorts, beaches, plenty of sunshine, spotting beautiful tropical birds, unusual tropical plants, and first class medical services by highly qualified specialists.

Area of Services Include:
- Cardiology - Angioplasty and Cardiac Bypass surgery
- Dentistry – dental implants, cleaning, whitening, dental surgery, etc.
- Dermatology
- Endoscopic Surgery
- ENT Surgery (Otorhinolaryngology) - Endoscopic nasal and microscopic ear surgeries
- Gastroenterology
- General Surgery - Laparoscopic removal of Gall Bladder stones and various abdominal tumors
- Haematology
- Interventional Radiology
- Maxillofacial and Oral Surgery
- Neurology (Neurosurgery) - Removal of Brain Tumour and slipped disk removal
- Nuclear Medicine
- Obstetrics and Gynaecology
- Oncology
- Ophtamology - Cataract, Glaucoma, Spectacle removal with lasers
- Orthopaedic Surgery - Knee and Hip replacement, Arthroscopy
- Orthodontics and Prosthetics
- Paediatric Surgery
- Periodontics
- Plastic and Reconstructive Surgery - Breast implants and Liposuction
- Thoracic/Vascular Surgery

- Trauma Surgery
- Rheumatology
- Spinal Surgery
- Urology - Prostate surgery and Penile implants
- Vascular Surgery

Price advantage is the driving force for medical tourism in South Africa. Your clients can obtain any of the above medical procedures/services at about 85% lower rate plus the sightseeing and the opportunity to visit another country.

For more details contact:

Serokolo Health Solutions (Pty) Ltd
Tel: +27 11 804 7117
Fax: +27 11 656 9378
Email: info@serokolo.co.za
Website: www.serokolo.co.za
       www.southafrica.net

India

Area of Services Include:
- Cardiology - Angioplasty and Cardiac Bypass surgery
- Dentistry – dental implants, cleaning, whitening, dental surgery, etc.
- Dermatology
- Endoscopic Surgery
- ENT Surgery (Otorhinolaryngology) - Endoscopic nasal and microscopic ear surgeries
- Gastroenterology
- General Surgery - Laparoscopic removal of Gall Bladder stones and various abdominal tumors
- Haematology
- Interventional Radiology
- Maxillofacial and Oral Surgery
- Neurology (Neurosurgery) - Removal of Brain Tumor and slipped disk removal
- Nuclear Medicine
- Obstetrics and Gynaecology
- Oncology
- Ophtamology - Cataract, Glaucoma, Spectacle removal with lasers
- Orthopaedic Surgery - Knee and Hip replacement, Arthroscopy
- Orthodontics and Prosthetics
- Paediatric Surgery
- Periodontics
- Plastic and Reconstructive Surgery - Breast implants and Liposuction
- Thoracic/Vascular Surgery
- Trauma Surgery

- Rheumatology
- Spinal Surgery
- Urology - Prostate surgery and Penile implants
- Vascular Surgery

Price advantage is the driving force for medical tourism in India. Your clients will obtain any of the above medical procedures/services at about 85% lower rate plus the sightseeing and the opportunity to visit another country.

For more details contact:

Advent Medical Services
667, Phase-II Mohali (India)
Fax - 0091-172-5095136 or 0091-172-5096324
Phone- 0091-9815888666
Website: http://www.hellomd.com
Randhawa Hospital
12, The Mall,
Amritsar,
INDIA
Tel: 91-183-2226660, or 91-183-2564039
Website: www.randhawahospital.com

Other Hospitals are:
- Apollo Hosptial
- B.M.Birla Heart Research Centre
- Christian Medical College
- Tata Memorial Hospital
- Apollo Cancer Hospital
- Indraprastha Medical Corporation
- Institute for Cardiovascular Diseases
- Escorts Hospital and Research Centre

Singapore

Contacts in Singapore:

Dr. Leslie Kuek
6, Napier road,
Gleneagles Medical Center
#03-08, Singapore 258499
Website: www.lesliekuekplasticsurgery.com

Parkway Group Healthcare
Medical Referral Centre (MRC)
302 Orchard Road
Tong Building #16-01/02/03

Singapore 238862
Tel: (65) 6735 5000 (24-hour hotline)
Fax: (65) 6732 6733
Website: www.imrc.com.sg

Raffles International Patients Centre
Raffles Hospital
585 North Bridge Road
Singapore 188770
Tel: (65) 6311 1666
Fax: (65) 6311 2333
Website: www.raffleshospital.com

National Healthcare Group International Patient Liaison Centre
National University Hospital
5 Lower Kent Ridge Road
Singapore 119074
Tel: (65) 6779 2777 (24-hour hotline)
Fax: (65) 6777 8065
Website: www.nuh.com.sg

Singapore Health Services (SingHealth) International Medical Service
Singapore General Hospital
Block 6 Level 1
Outram Road
Singapore 169608
Tel: (65) 6326 5656
Fax: (65) 6326 5900

Thailand
Website: www.medicaltourisminthailand.com

The Philippines

Manila Doctors Hospital, United Nations Ave., Manila
World City Medical Center, Aurora Blvd., Quezon City
Golden Gate Hospital, Batangas City
St. Patrick's Hospital, Batangas City
Website: www.cosmeticsurgeryphil.com

EYE REPUBLIC Ophthalmology Clinic
3/F Don Santiago Building Unit 310
1344 Taft Avenue, Ermita
Manila, Philippines 1000
Telefax: (+632) 536-2398

Trunk: (+632) 523-8271 to 79 local 30
Mobile: (+63917) 899-2020
Website: www.medicaltourism.ph

Malaysia

Sunway Medical Center
No.5, Jalan Lagoon Selatan, Bandar Sunway,
46150 Petaling Jaya, Selangor Darul Ehsan.
Tel: 03-7491 9191
Fax: 03-7491 8181
Website: www.sunway.com.my

General
www.medicaltourism.com

Before recommending a hospital and package for your clients, you have to verify:

- Whether there is a specialist for the procedure your client requires
- The qualification/credentials of the specialist
  The credentials and track record of the hospital
- That the hospital has all the necessary equipment for the procedure

CHECK WITH THE NATIONAL ASSOCIATION OF SURGEONS IN EACH COUNTRY TO SEE STATUS OF EACH SPECIALIST AND HOSPITAL WITH THE ASSOCIATION.

The above steps are necessary because, in some of the above mentioned countries that offer medical tourism, there are weak medical malpractice laws, and you and your patients wouldn't have a sustainable recourse to local courts or medical boards if anything went wrong.

It is also good to check so that complications, side-effects and post-operative care are reduced, because they will become the responsibility of the medical care system in the patients' home countries.

What You Need To Start Up:

For an effective tour operating business, you need the tour operator's software. Some of these software systems cover the A to Z: all aspects of inbound and outbound tour operation.
Visit the website: www.caterra.com/tour-operating-software
You will have a list of over 45 Tour Operating Software.

- A Computer (with Internet connection)
  Use a desktop or a laptop computer with a 56k modem. Install the following

software on the computer:

- o **Word processor (MS Office) -** Use this to write letters, create mailing labels, and address envelopes. In the MS Office you've got MS Word, Excel, Access, Outlook, and PowerPoint.
- o **Spreadsheet** - You can create charts and do your finances with a spreadsheet program. Use MS Excel for your spreadsheet needs.
- o **QuickBooks Pro** - With this, you can create custom invoices, compute sales, do electronic banking, pay your bills, control your inventory and payroll. Use it for all accounting and bookkeeping.
- o **Database** - Use a database program to keep records of clients, sellers, vendors and all your business contacts/links. With the database program, you can keep records of phone calls, faxes, meetings, conferences and seminars, and note time and dates of events and incidents. You may want to use MS Access, Dbase or Fox Pro for your database needs.
- o **Graphic** - Use this to create flyers, announcements newsletters and advertisements. You may want to use PageMaker, QuarkXpress and ClarisWorks for your graphic exploits.
- o **Scheduler** - Use this to manage your schedules.
- Phone, Fax, Printer, Scanner, Copier (can buy all-in-one)
- Office Furniture (including office supplies and office accessories)
- Digital photo camera
- Video camera (digital preferably)
- Insurance
- Fees payable to become a member in professional and or trade associations.
- Books
- Marketing/advertising cost.

Professional/Trade Associations You May Like To Join/Know:

Travel Clinics Across Canada

International Association for Medical Assistance to Travellers
CANADA
40 Regal Road
Guelph, Ontario
N1K 1B5
Tel: 519 836 0102
Fax: 519 836 3412
OR
1287 St. Clair Avenue West, Suite #1
Toronto, Ontario
M6E 1B8
Tel: 416 652 0137

USA
IAMAT
1623 Military Rd. #279
Niagara Falls, NY 14304-1745
Tel: 716 754 4883

World Federation of Tourist Guide Association Head Office
The WFTGA Administrator,
Wirtschaftskammer Wien
FG Freizeitbetriebe
Judenplats 3 - 4
1010 Wien
Austria
Phone: 43-1-51450 4211
Fax: 43-1-51450 4216
Email: info@wftga.org
Website: www.wftga.org
Representative of the Federation in Canada
Houri Nazaretian
1363 wecker Drive
Oshawa, On
L1J 3P8
Phone: 905-721-0783
Fax; 905-721-9062
Email; knazaretia@aol.com

Canadian Tour Guide Association of Toronto
122-250, The East Mall, Suite 1705
Toronto, On
M9B 6L3
Phone: 416-410-8621
Fax: 416-410-8621
Email; info@ctgaoftoronto.rg
Website: www.ctgaoftoronto.org

Association des Guides Touristiques des Quebec Inc.
College Merici
Case Postale 79
755, Chemin St.-Louis
Quebec City, QC
G1S 1C1

The Alberta Tour Directors Association
Box 8044
Canmore, AB
T1W 2T8

Phone: 403-678-2833
Email: ctconsultants@monarc.net
Contact: Alison Day

Association Professionalle des Guides Touristiques
Chapitre de Montreal (APGT)
C.P. 982, Succursale Place d'Armes
Montreal, QC
H2Y 3J4
Phone: 514-990-9849
Email: renelemieuxguide@hotmail.com
Contact: Rene Lemieux
Website: www.apgtmontreal.org

Canadian tour Guides Association of British Columbia
BOX 2440
Vancouver, BC
V6B 3W7
Phone: 604-876-2576
Fax: 604-872-2640
Email: jeff@ctgaofbc.com
Contact: Jeff Veniot
Website: www.ctgaofbc.com

Capital Tour Guide Association
496 Parkdale Ave.
Ottawa, On
K1Y 0A3
Phone: 613-722-5939
Fax: 613-722-5743
Contact: Lenore Leon

Books you May Need to Buy:

Books for tour management and marketing

Conducting Tours: A Practical Guide
Published by Thomas Delmar learning
Author: Marc Mancini, Terri Gaylord
ISBN: 076681419X

Start Your Own Specialty Travel & Tour Business
Published by Self-Counsel Press
Author: Barbara Braidwood
ISBN: 1551802848

Successful International Tour Director: How To Become an International Tour Director
Published by Authors Choice Press
Author: Geralde Mitchell
ISBN: 0595167020

Internet Marketing For Your Tourism Business: Proven Techniques For Promoting Tourist Based Business Over The Internet
Published by Maximum Press
Author: Susan Sweeney
ISBN: 1885068476

Becoming A Tour Guide: The Principles of Guiding and Site Interpretation
Published by Int. Thomson Business Press
Author: Verite Reily Collins
ISBN: 0826447880

The Professional Guide: Dynamics of Tour Guiding
Published by Wiley
Author: Kathleen Lingle Pond
ISBN: 047128386X

Essentials of Tour Management
Published by Prentice hall
Author: Betsy Fay
ISBN: 0132850656

The Good Guide: A Sourcebook For Interpreters, Docents, And Tour Guides
Published by Ironwood Press
Author: Alison L. Grinder
ISBN: 0932541003

Selling Destinations: Geography For The Travel Professional
Published by Delmar Thompson Learning
Author: Marc Mancini
ISBN: 1401819826

How To Start A Home-Based Travel Agency
Published by Tom Ogg and Associates
Author: Tom Ogg
ISBN: 1888290056

Guerrilla Publicity
Published by Adams Media Corporation
Author: Jay Conrad Levinson, Rich Frishman, Jill Lublin
ISBN: 1-58062-682-3

Marketing Without Advertising
Author: Michael Phillips, Salli Rasberry
ISBN: 0873376080

The 22 Immutable Laws of Marketing
Published by Harper Business
Author: Al Ries and Jack Trout
ISBN: 0887306667

6 Steps To Free Publicity
Published by Career Press Inc
Author: Marcia Yudkin
ISBN: 1-56414-675-8

Endless Referrals: Network Your Everyday Contacts into Sales (New and Updated Edition)
Author: Bob Burg
ISBN: 0070089973

How To Become Your Own Publicist
Published by McGraw-Hill
Author: Jessica Hatchigan
ISBN:0-07-138332-8

Marketing/How To Get Business

Hunting for business for your Medical Tourism Business is about the same as searching for a job in your field. As such, you have to apply all the job search skills you have acquired over the years, customizing them to suit your present need and position.

- Cold calls to Schools, Organizations and Conference/Convention Organizers for information and interviews about who may need the services, and to provide them with reasons they may need the services of your Tour Operating/Management Firm.
- Network with medical professionals, hospitals, treatment facilities, hotels and tour operators.
- Network with other tour operators nationally and internationally - including tour operators in your country of origin and countries around it. You can be exchanging tour packages and sending and receiving tourist groups to and from these countries.
- Yellow Pages advertisement
- Brochure/Flyers
- Business Cards
- Create a Website
- Associations/Social Clubs
- Distribute gift certificates and discounted tour packages to your clients to

give to their friends

- Send out tour package offers for special days and seasons like Christmas, New Year, Easter, Canada Day, Valentine's Day, etc.
- Keep in touch with your clients and call the clients who have not used your services for some time to remind them of your good services and any new discounted offers available.
- Find out and incorporate the marketing methods and approaches of other professionals in your field into your own method and approach.
- Call your clients - new/old/regular, a day or two after they use your services to thank them for using the services of your tour management firm, but above all, to ask them how they are feeling, and if they enjoyed the trip.
- Offer discounts to your regular clients and offer them a free tour package if they bring in four or more new clients - referral reward
- Send out a discounted tour package offer for students, seniors, couples, singles, teenagers, and some specific professionals like lawyers, truck drivers, factory workers, teachers etc, including a lecture session on a particular topic.
- Develop a weekly newsletter or write in the local newspaper and or magazine giving tips on how to increase awareness, enrich one's cultural sense, love and promote the environment and cultural heritage, and use tours and sightseeing to manage stress.
- Encourage people to express their views on healthcare/wellness/alternative healing, and have your patients share their stories with others, on the radios, in newspapers and on television.

Good luck!

Chapter 17

MICROBREWERY

Beer brewing dates back about 10,000 years, when people fermented grains at home. The term, "Microbrew" dates back to the late 60's and early 70's. Microwbrewers are small producers of beer that serve local and regional consumers. Brewpubs are extensions of microbreweries. Brewpubs brew their own beer and sell it in their own local pubs. Small local brewery is therefore not a new idea.

In the present day world, with the increase in designer labels and organic edibles, people are edging towards their own brands of drinks, away from the regular mass-produced and canned drinks. Microbrewing is on the rise because people, after consuming micro-brewed beer, do not want to go back to the bland canned beer brands flooded with chemicals and additives. Micro-brewed beers, has better taste and flavour and is far more robust than major brands.

To start and run a microbrewery is not as difficult as you might think. It is actually easy and profitable. You can use hundreds of books, websites, and guides on how to start, run brew and own your own microbrewery. All you need is research, some experimenting with various varieties and tastes, recipes and instructions, and who knows, you may shout eureka to the next great beer.

To qualify as a microbrewery, you must be producing less than 15,000 barrels (approximately 179,000 decalitres) of beer annually.

Basic Procedure you need to make you beer includes:
- Following recipe and instructions that are included with your supply/ equipment to make your beer your way.
- Follow ingredient measurements in the guide book
- Combine ingredients and initiate fermentation
- Transfer the fermented beer from the primary fermenter to a secondary fermenter
- Transfer from the secondary fermenter to the container of choice – bottles, etc
- Bottle, cap and store for further maturation, aging and classification
- Good sanitary conditions must abound
- Remember that beer brewing is temperature sensitive

Some types of beers you may like to brew include:
Ales, Lagers, Bitters, Light beers, Pilsners, Porter, Stouts etc
You may want to specialize in one, two or all of the beer types.

Some Useful websites for your Equipment, Ingredient Supplies and Resources:
- www.brewbeeryourself.com
- www.home-brew.com
- www.austinhomebrew.com
- www.eckraus.com
- www.store.yahoo.com
- www.plowandhearth.com
- www.thegrape.net
- www.wineartindy.com
- www.electrolab.biz
- www.allaboutbeer.com
- www.beerinfo.com
- www.beerbooks.com
- www.allthebrands.com
- www.mrbeer.com
- www.homebrewbook.com
- www.howtobrew.com
- www.realbrew.com
- www.morebeer.com
- www.beer-brewing.com
- www.beer-brewing.discoveryweb.net
- www.homebrewtalk.com/
- www.realbeer.com/caba

What You Need To Start-Up
- Instruction Books
- Ingredients: Beer yeast, Hops, Malt extract, Sugar, Grain, Clarifying agent, Water, Flavours, etc.
- Equipment: Space (3x3feet, 5x5 feet, 8x8 feet, depending on the size of your brewery), Boiling Kettle or Pot, Source of Heat, Primary Fermenters, Secondary Fermenters, Fermenting Bottles, Cans, Drums, Crowns Air Lock, Rubber Stopper, Siphoning and Transferring Equipment, Long-handled Mixing Spoon, thermometer, Sanitizing and Clearing Solutions, Recappable beer bottles, Crown Cappers, Wort Cooler, labels, Hydrometer.
- A Computer (with Internet connection)

  Use a desktop or a laptop computer with a 56k modem. Install the following software on the computer:
  - **Word processor (MS Office) -** Use this to write letters, create mailing labels, and address envelopes. In the MS Office you've got MS Word, Excel, Access, Outlook, and PowerPoint.
  - **Spreadsheet** - You can create charts and do your finances with a

spreadsheet program. Use MS Excel for your spreadsheet needs.

o **QuickBooks Pro** - With this, you can create custom invoices, compute sales, do electronic banking, pay your bills, control your inventory and payroll. Use it for all accounting and bookkeeping.

o **Database** - Use a database program to keep records of clients, sellers, vendors and all your business contacts/links. With the database program, you can keep records of phone calls, faxes, meetings, conferences and seminars, and note time and dates of events and incidents. You may want to use MS Access, Dbase or Fox Pro for your database needs.

o **Graphic** - Use this to create flyers, announcements newsletters and advertisements. You may want to use PageMaker, QuarkXpress and ClarisWorks for your graphic exploits.

o **Scheduler** - Use this to manage your schedules.

- Phone, Fax, Printer, Scanner, Copier (can buy all-in-one)
- Office Furniture (including office supplies and office accessories)
- Insurance
- Fees payable to become a member in professional and or trade associations.
- Books
- Marketing/advertising cost.

Professional Associations You May Like To Join/Know:

Brewers Association Of Canada
650-100 Queen Street
Ottawa, Ontario
K1P 1J9
Phone: 613-232-9601
Fax: 613-232-2283
Website: www.brewers.ca
Email: info@brewers.ca

Canadian Amateur Brewers Association.
Contact: Richard Oluszak
2255 B Queen St. East, Suite 749
Toronto Ontario
M4E1G3 Canada
Phone: 416/812-6732
Fax: 416/690-2055
E-Mail: eamonn@atmosp.pyhics.utoronto.ca
Newsletter E-mail: darryl@sagedesign.com
Website: www.homebrewers.ca
This association promotes and encourage home and micro-brewers through educational seminars, workshops and publications. The association encourages new microbrewers with new techniques and networking with club affiliations in and around Canada.

Edmonton Home Brewing Guild
Edmonton, Alberta
Canada
Website: www.compusmart.ab.ca/

Saskatoon A.L.E.S. (Ale and Lager Enthusiasts of Saskatchewan)
Contact: Mark Nedoly
#106-185, 3120 8th St., E.
Saskatoon, SK
S7H OW2 Canada
Website: www.alesclub.com
E-Mail: mtn290@mail.usask.ca

Members of Barleyment (MOB)
Website: www.barleyment.wort.ca
MontreAlers
Website: www.montrealers.ca
The Brewnosers
Website: http://www.chebucto.ns.ca/Recreation/BrewNoser/

The Calgary Association Of Home-Brewers (Marquis de Suds)

The Vinyard Wine and Beer Making Supplies
#101, 5403 Crowchild Trail NW
Calgary, Alberta
T3B 4Z1
Phone: 403-288-7775
Website: http://members.shaw.ca/markafox/

MeadWorks Brewing Club Vancouver
Website: www.meadworks.ca
Washington (USA)

Bainbridge Island Brewers (The Yeasty Boys)
Contact: Fred Parst
14140 Sunrise Drive
Bainbridge Island, WA 98110
Phone: 206/780-0988
E-Mail: pabstcan@jps.net

Boeing Employees Wine And Beer Makers Club
Contact: Al Cutshall
6608 118th Ave., S.E.
Bellvue, WA 98006
Phone: 253/773-8737
E-Mail: alden.d.cutshall@boeing.com

Cascade Brewers Guild
Contact: Tim O'Brian & Jeannie McWilliams
16625 Redmond Way, Suite M-400
Redmond, WA 98052
Phone: 425-868-0325
E-Mail: Jeanniem@carecomputer.com
E-Mail: timob@msn.com
Website: www.nwmarket.com/cbg

Greater Everett Breweries League
Contact: Shelly Albright
18623 40th Place, NE
Snohomish, WA 98290
Phone: 360-691-7042
E-Mail: salbrigh@eskimo.com

New York
   Brewers In Endicott Region (BIER)
   Contact: Dave King
   617 Leaon Dr.
   Endicott, NY 13760
   Phone: 607/748-6904
   E-Mail: dking99@aol.com

   Long Islanders for Fermentation Enjoyment (L.I.F.E.)
   Contact: Marc Arkind
   P.O. Box 712
   Hicksville, NY 11802-0712
   Phone: 516/932-1090
   Fax: 516/932-1099 E-Mail: alpine82@rols.com

Michigan (USA)
   The Choir Boys
   Contact: David Reneaud
   219 N. Saginaw
   Byron, MI. 48418
   Phone: 810/560-1204 or 810/266-6166
   E-Mail: dreneaud@juno.com

   C.R.A.F.T.
   Contact: Liz Wilson
   127 Huron
   Mt. Clemens, MI 48043
   Phone: 810/465-7314
   Fax: 810/469-4860
   E-Mail: ewilson127@juno.com

URL: www.angelfire.com/mi/craftbrewclub/index.html

The Detroit Carboys
Contact: Ed Marsh
P.O. Box 1585
Royal Oak, MI. 48068-1585
Phone: 248/399-4186
Fax: 248/548-1176

The Fermental Order of Renaissance Draughtsmen (FORD)
Contact: Pat Babcock
2478 Cabot Rd.
Canton Township, MI 48188-1825
E-Mail: pbabcock@hbd.org

Gitchi Guumee south Shore Brewers
Contact: Daniel Bowling
34793 County Road 581
Ishpemming, MI 49849
Phone: 906/485-6111
E-Mail: dabowl@up.net
Website: www.angelfire.com/mi/mqtbrewers

The Computerized Homebrew Avocation and Obsession Society (CHAOS)
Contact: Pat Babcock
2478 Cabot Road
Canton Township, MI 48188-1825
E-Mail: pbabcock@hbd.org
Website: http://hbd.org/chaos

Books You May Need To Buy:

Radical Brewing: Recipes, Tales & World-Altering Meditations in a Glass
By Randy Mosher
Publisher: Brewers Publications, 2004.

Complete Joy of Homebrewing, 3rd Edition
By Charlie Papazian
Publisher: Harper Resource, 2003.

101 Ideas For Homebrew Fun
By Ray Daniels
Publisher: Brewers Publications, 1998.

A Year of Beer: 260 Seasonal Homebrew Recipes
By Amahl Turczyn
Publisher: Brewers Publications, 1997.

Beer Captured: Homebrew Recipes For 150 World Class Brews
By Tess and Mark Szamatulski
Publisher: Maltose Press, 2001.

Brew Chem 101: The Basics of Homebrewing Chemistry
By Lee W. Janson, Ph.D.
Publisher: Storey Books, 1996

Brew Classic European Beers At Home
By Graham Wheeler and Roger Protz
Publisher: CAMRA Books, 1997.

Brew Ware: How To Find, Adapt & Build Homebrewing Equipment
By Karl F. Lutzen & Mark Stevens
Publisher: Storey Books, 1996.

Brewing Made Easy: From The First Batch To Creating Your Own Recipes
By Joe Fisher & Dennis Fisher
Publisher: Storey Books, 1996.

The Brewmaster's Bible: The Gold Standard for Homebrewers
By Stephen Snyder
Publisher: Harper Perennial, 1997.

Clone Brews: Homebrew Recipes for 150 Commercial Beers
By Tess and Mark Szamatulski
Publisher: Storey Books, 1998.

Dave Miller's Homebrewing Guide: Everything You Need To Know To Make Great-Tasting Beer
By Dave Miller
Publisher: Storey Books, 1995.

Designing Great Beers: The Ultimate Guide to Brewing Classic Beer Styles
By Ray Daniels
Publisher: Brewers Publications, 1996.

Homebrewer's Companion
By Charlie Papazian
Publisher: Harper Resource, 2003.

Home Brewer's Recipe Database: Ingredient Information for Over Two Thousand

Commercial European Beers
By Les Howarth
Publisher: iUniverse Star, 2004.

Dictionary of Beer & Brewing: All New Revised Second Edition
By Dan Rabin and Carl Forget
Publisher: Brewers Publications, 1998.

Homebrewing For Dummies
By Marty Nachel
Publisher: IDG Books, 1997.

New Brewing Lager Beer: The Most Comprehensive Book for Home- and Microbrewers
By Gregory J. Noonan
Publisher: Brewers Publications, 2003.

North American Clone Brews: Homebrew Recipes for Your Favorite American & Canadian Beers
By Scott R. Russell
Publisher: Storey Books, 2000.

Brewers Handbook: Complete Beer Brewing Instructions

Books For Marketing:

Guerrilla Publicity
Published by Adams Media Corporation
Author: Jay Conrad Levinson, Rich Frishman, and Jill Lublin
ISBN: 1-58062-682-3

Marketing Without Advertising
Author: Michael Phillips, Salli Rasberry
ISBN: 0873376080

The 22 Immutable Laws of Marketing
Published by Harper Business
Author: Al Ries and Jack Trout
ISBN: 0887306667

The 22 Irrefutable Laws of Advertising
Published by John Willey and Sons
Author: Michael Newman
ISBN: 0470-82106-X

6 Steps To Free Publicity
Published by Career Press Inc
Author: Marcia Yudkin
ISBN: 1-56414-675-8

Endless Referrals: Network Your Everyday Contacts into Sales (New and Updated Edition)
Author: Bob Burg
ISBN: 0070089973

How To Become Your Own Publicist
Published by McGraw-Hill
Author: Jessica Hatchigan
ISBN: 0-07-138332-8

Guerrilla Selling: Unconventional Weapons and Tactics for Increasing Your Sales
Published by Houghton Mifflin
Author: Bill Gallagher, Orvel Ray Wilson and Jay Conrad Levinson
ISBN: 0395580390

Guerrilla Teleselling: New Unconventional Weapons and Tactics To Sell When You Can't Be There in Person
Author: Jay Conrad Levinson, Mark S.A Smith, and Orval Ray Wilson
ISBN: 0471242799

How To Become A Marketing Superstar
Published by Hyperion Books
Author: Jeffrey J. Fox
ISBN: 0-7868-6824-4

Marketing/ How To Get Business
- Find out and incorporate the marketing methods and approaches of other professionals in your field into your own method and approach
- Network with other professionals who are into private practise in your professional Organization to find out who needs a plug for his expertise and practise.
- Yellow pages advertisement
- Brochure/Flyers
- Business Cards
- Create a Website
- Join Associations/Social Clubs
- Distribute gift certificates and discounted publicity packages to clients to give to their friends
- Send out publicity package offers for special days and seasons like Christmas, New year, Easter, Canada Day, Valentine's day, etc.

- Offer free publicity package to your regular clients for referrals
- Develop a weekly/monthly Newsletter, write in the local newspaper and or magazine giving tips on tasty beer without chemicals and additives.

Good luck!

Chapter 18

TRANSLATOR/INTERPRETER

Every year companies and organisations dollars to have documents and text translated into languages other than English language.

Some people learn to speak, or come from non-English/non-French speaking countries and or countries that speak English/French and other languages like: Portuguese, Spanish, Russian, Hindi, Punjabi, Urdu, Igbo, Afghan, Chinese, Swahili, Japanese, Vietnamese, Bosnian, Romanian, Czech, Zulu, Ukrainian, Arabic, Pakistani, Polish, Korean, Taiwanese, Thai language, etc.

The ability to speak one and or more of these languages in addition to speaking English/French language is the foremost requirement in becoming a translator/interpreter.

Possible areas of Translation work:
- Documents (official and unofficial)
- Films/Videos
- Books - prose/poetry
- Technical texts
- Website text content

As a translator, you must be clear and concise, using the exact meaning of words in translating.

Possible Places for Interpretation work:
- Seminars
- Law courts
- Conferences
- Churches
- Rallies
- Airports/Seaports/Land borders

Translating and Interpreting in some areas may need Certification and or License.

As a translator/interpreter, you need to have a good knowledge of the two languages in question. You may also subcontract other translators. In technical text translating, it is always advisable to have a technical knowledge in the field of the text.

What You need To Start-Up

- A Computer (with Internet connection)

  Use a desktop or a laptop computer with a 56k modem. Install the following software on the computer:
  - o **Word processor (MS Office) -** Use this to write letters, create mailing labels, and address envelopes. In the MS Office you've got MS Word, Excel, Access, Outlook, and PowerPoint.
  - o **Spreadsheet** - You can create charts and do your finances with a spreadsheet program. Use MS Excel for your spreadsheet needs.
  - o **QuickBooks Pro** - With this, you can create custom invoices, compute sales, do electronic banking, pay your bills, control your inventory and payroll. Use it for all accounting and bookkeeping.
  - o **Database** - Use a database program to keep records of clients, sellers, vendors and all your business contacts/links. With the database program, you can keep records of phone calls, faxes, meetings, conferences and seminars, and note time and dates of events and incidents. You may want to use MS Access, Dbase or Fox Pro for your database needs.
  - o **Graphic** - Use this to create flyers, announcements newsletters and advertisements. You may want to use PageMaker, QuarkXpress and ClarisWorks for your graphic exploits.
  - o **Scheduler** - Use this to manage your schedules.
- Phone, Fax, Printer, Scanner, Copier (can buy all-in-one)
- Office Furniture (including office supplies and office accessories)
- Insurance
- Fees payable to become a member in professional and or trade associations.
- Books
- Marketing/advertising cost.
- Business suits, ties, shoes, briefcase (all for personal image improvement) and other miscellaneous expenses

You may also want to have your Translation firm Online. In that case you may need to implement the steps for establishing a business Online as explained in the 'Steps for Establishing a Business Online' section of this book.

The total cost of your start-up needs will not exceed $20,000 Canadian.

Professional/Trade Associations/Organizations You May Like To Join/Know:

Canadian Translators and Interpreters Council (CTIC)
This is an umbrella organization for the provincial and territorial associations of British Columbia, Alberta, New Brunswick, Nova Scotia, Newfoundland and Labrador, the Northwest Territories, Nunavut, Manitoba, Ontario, Quebec, Saskatchewan and the Yukon.

Association of Translators and Interpreters of Ontario (ATIO)
Phone: 613-241-2846
Toll free: 1-800-234-5030
Website: www.atio.on.ca

Association of Translators and Interpreters of Manitoba (ATIM)
200 Ave de la Cathedrale, BOX 83
Winnipeg, Manitoba
R2H 0H7
Phone: 204-797-3247
Email: info@atim.mb.ca
Website: www.atim.mb.ca

Association of Translators and Interpreters of Alberta (ATIA)
P.O.BOX 546
Main Post Office
Edmonton, Alberta
T5J 2K8
Phone: 780-434-8384
Website: www.atia.ab.ca

Society of Translators and Interpreters of British Columbia (STIBC)
Website: www.stibc.org

Translators and Interpreters association of Quebec
Ordre des Traducteurs et Interpretes Agrees du Quebec (OTIAQ)
Website: www.otiaq.org

Association of Visual Language Interpreters of Canada
Website: www.avlic.ca

Association of Translators and Interpreters of Saskatchewan (ATISK)
Website: www.atis-sk.ca

Canadian Translators, Terminologists and Interpreters Council
Website: www.cttic.org

Corporation of Translators, Terminologists and Interpreters of New Brunswick
Website: www.ctinb.nb.ca

Literary Translators Association of Canada
Website: www.geocities.com

Network of Translators in Education
Website: www.rte-net.ca

The Nunavut Interpreters and Translators Society
Website: www.nunanet.com

American Translators Association
Website: www.atanet.org
On this site you may learn one or two things about the translation and interpretation profession.

Institute of Translation and Interpreting
Website: www.iti.org.uk
In this site you may find some basic start-up information for interpreters and translators.

Foreign Language Forum on Compuserve
Website: www.go.compuserve.com/foreignlanguage

International Association of Conference Interpreters
10 Avenue de Secheron--Ch,
1202 Geneva, Switzerland.
Website: www.aiic.net

Marketing/How To Get Business

Hunting for business for your Translation/Interpreter firm is about the same as searching for a job in your field. As such, you have to apply all the job search skills you have acquired over the years, customizing them to suit your present need and position.

- Cold calls to Companies, Businesses that engage in international transactions, Organisations, Law firms, Immigration offices, Seminar/ Conference/Rally Organizers and or churches for information and interviews about who may need your services, and to provide them with reasons they may need the services of your Firm.
- Networking
- Yellow pages advertisement
- Brochure/Flyers
- Business Cards
- Create a Website
- Join Associations/social clubs
- Trade fairs

Good luck!

Chapter 19

ONLINE FLORIST/GIFT SHOP

Emotion is indigenous to man. Emotion, the manifestation of emotion and the tangible exchange of emotion is as old as mankind. Ferrying the tangible expression of peoples emotion can be a lovely and interesting business.

Online business has been described by lots of people as "the gold rush of the present century". And joining this razzle of 'gold rush' by transporting the tangible expression of people's lovely emotions and passion couldn't be more dazzling.

As an online florist/gift shop owner, you do not handle, take care of or stock flowers, plants and gift items. You make arrangements with traditional florists (flower shop owners) and gift shop owners for supply. But, nevertheless, you need to have a good knowledge of flowers and gift items.

For setting up your flower/gift shop online, see the section of this book that explains the 'Steps For Establishing a Business Online in Chapter 3'. In addition, you will need:
- Phone, Fax, Printer, Scanner, Copier (can buy all-in-one)
- Office Furniture (including office supplies and office accessories)
- Insurance
- Fees payable to become a member in professional and or trade associations (if any).
- Books
- Marketing/advertising cost and other miscellaneous expenses.
- Digital photo Camera

The total cost of your start-up needs will not exceed $20,000 Canadian.

Books You May Need To Buy:

The Unofficial Guide to Starting a Business Online
Published by Wiley Publishing, Inc.
Author: Jason R. Rich
ISBN0-02-863340-7

Doing Big Business on the Internet
Published by Self-Counsel Press

Author: Hurley & Birkwood
ISBN: 1-55180-119-1

Selling On The Web
Author: Paul Galloway
ISBN: 1563824876

Start an eBay Business
Published by Alpha Books
Author: Barbara Weltman
ISBN: 159257-333-9

Small Business Online
A Strategic Guide for Canada Entrepreneurs
Published by Prentice Hall Canada Inc.
Author: Jim Carroll with Rich Broadhead
ISBN: 0-13-976895-5

101 Ways To Promote your Website
Published by Maximum Press
Author: Susan Sweeney
ISBN: 1931644217

Start Your Own Business On eBay: Your Step by Step Guide To Success
Published by Entrepreneur Press
Author: Jacquelyn Lynn
ISBN: 1932531122

Start Your Own E-Business
Published by Entrepreneur Press
Author: Entrepreneur Press
ISBN: 1932156747

Selling On The Net: The Complete Guide
Published by NTC Business Books
Author: Lewis, Herschell Gordon
ISBN: 0844232343

Selling On The Internet: How To Open An Electronic Storefront And Have Millions Of Customers Come To You
Published by McGraw-Hill
Author: James C. Gonyea, Wayne M. Gonyea
ISBN: 0070241872

The Online Business Book
Published by Adam Media Corporation

Author: Rob Liflander
ISBN: 158062-3204

Guerrilla Marketing Online
Published by Houghton Mifflin
Author: Jay Conrad Levinson and Charles Rubin
ISBN: 0-395-86061-X

Internet Marketing For Dummies
Published by Wiley Publishing Inc.,
ISBN: 0-7645-0778-8

Low-Cost Website Promotion
Published by Adam Media Corporation
Author: Barry Feig
ISBN: 1-58062-501-0

Online Business Resources
Published by Made E-Z
Author: Paul Galloway
ISBN: 1-56382-510-4

Generating Trust in Online Business: From Theory To Practice
Published by IQ
Author: Magda Fusaro
ISBN: 2-922417-28-X

Absolute Beginners Guide to Launching an eBay Business
Published by Que
Author: Micheal Miller
ISBN: 0-7897-3058-8

Starting an eBay Business For Dummies
Published by Wiley Publishing Inc.,
Author: Marsha Collier
ISBN: 0-7645-6924-4

Online Business Planning
Published by Career Press
Author: Robert T. Gorman
ISBN: 1-56414-369-4

Marketing Without Advertising
Author: Michael Phillips, Salli Rasberry
ISBN: 0873376080

Guerrilla Publicity
Published by Adams Media Corporation
Author: Jay Conrad Levinson, Rich Frishman, Jill Lublin
ISBN: 1-58062-682-3

Visit the following websites to get an idea of what your own site may look like:
- www.1800flowers.com
- www.proflowers.com
- www.ftd.com
- www.floristconnection.com
- www.flowersshope.com
- www.fromyouflowers.com
- www.800flowerdelivery.com
- www.coasttocoastflorist.com
- www.flowerdelivery.com
- www.secure.strawberrynet.com
- www.londonflowernet.com

Although the traditional florists with whom you make arrangement for the supplies will handle everything from floral design and arrangement, techniques, to the proper care and handling of fresh cut flowers, you may need to know/take lessons in:

Design Forms
In floral design forms, you will learn design forms including the symmetrical triangle, Circular, Asymmetrical triangle, Vertical, Oval, Fan shape, Crescent & Hogarth curve and European tied Bouquet styles.

Design Techniques
In design techniques, you will learn Basing, Focal Area, Terracing, Grouping, Clustering, Zoning, Banding, Binding, Shadowing, Framing & Parallelism, Colour Harmony and new experimental design styles.

Proper Care and Handling of Fresh Cut Flowers
In Care and Handling, you will learn the processing of freshly cut flowers, merchandising, flower & plant identification, and the availability of flowers and plants in the Canadian market.

Wedding Etiquette
In wedding etiquette, you will learn wedding order procedures, wiring and taping techniques, preparing a Brides Bouquet, Bridesmaids, Maid of Honour, flower gifts, how to set up flowers for a wedding ceremony and reception, Corsages and Boutonnieres.

Funerals and Sympathy Tributes
In Funeral and Sympathy Tributes, you will learn the step-by-step construction of Funeral baskets, Casket sprays, Standing sprays, Vase arrangements, Wreaths, Hearts

and Crosses, proper pricing and delivery.

Supply Channels
In this study, you will visit wholesale florists, where you will see large selections of fresh, silk and dried flowers. You will see all sorts of flowers including Orchids, tropical flowers and plants, hybrids, gift baskets, Vases etc.
This program will have a total duration of about three weeks.

Possible places to obtain this training include:

Canadian Institute of Floral Design
2794A Lakeshore Blvd. W.
Unit #3
Toronto, Ontario
M8V 1H5
Phone: 416-733-2387
Toll Free: 1-877-285-1931
Fax: 416-733-2387
Website: www.proflorists.net/
Outside Toronto and Ontario, look around for a floral design school in your area.

Marketing/How to Get Business
- Promote your website to increase the number of visitors to the website
- Advertise your website in the Yellow pages, newspapers and magazines
- Create brochures and flyers
- Business cards
- Look for corporate contracts in offices, schools, establishments and or Churches - a good source for knowing up coming weddings
- Organize/join a flower club
- Organize/join a birthday club
- Reach for Funeral houses, Hospitals, and event organizers

Good luck!

Chapter 20

DATING CLUB

This is the business of facilitating the meeting of people with mutual attraction to fulfill each other's emotional needs, making it possible for them to explore the depths of a relationship.

As a dating club operator, your business is practically linking people with people. As such, you need to be people smart, outgoing and warm, have knowledge of horoscope, Zodiac signs and harmony.

As a dating club operator, you may undertake:
- Live Speed Dating
- Online Speed Dating
- Personal Introduction Service
- Matchmaking
- Parties/Social Events
- Dance Classes
- Singles Dance Parties
- Garden Parties

How Live Speed Dating works

The dating club, using its marketing channel or membership pool, invites about 40 or more people (20 males and 20 females) for a price of $40 or more each. The meeting takes place in a hotel, bar, pub, restaurant and or banquet room. Each invitee will be given a card, pen or pencil to mark the tag number of each person he/she meets. Each and every male invitee will be given an opportunity to sit with each and every female invitee, and vice versa, for a maximum period of time - say ten minutes. If he/she likes the person, she/he marks his/her tag number on the card. The whole thing will be going on amidst music, entertainment, refreshment, side attractions etc. At the end of the day, everybody turns in his/her card, and the people are free to mingle normally. The dating club will then sort out the cards to find out which pairs have chemistry, and notify them by e-mail, phone, fax, or in writing. The club may give a follow-up help by inviting the pair to dance classes for a price, or inviting them to singles parties until they make a total nuptial take off.

Online Dating

People pay their membership dues and help themselves online. The dating club also helps find matches for members.

What You Need To Start-up

To set up your dating club, you will need to visit the section of this book that explains the 'Steps for setting up your business Online'. In addition, you need:
- Phone, fax, printer, Scanner, Copier (can buy all-in-one)
- Office furniture (including office supplies and office accessories)
- Insurance
- Digital Photo Camera
- Marketing/Advertising cost and other miscellaneous expenses

The total cost of your start-up need will not exceed $20,000 Canadian

Books you may Need:

The Unofficial Guide to Starting a Business Online
Published by Wiley Publishing, Inc.
Author: Jason R. Rich
ISBN0-02-863340-7

Doing Big Business on the Internet
Published by Self-Counsel Press
Author: Hurley & Birkwood
ISBN: 1-55180-119-1

Selling On The Web
Author: Paul Galloway
ISBN: 1563824876

Start an eBay Business
Published by Alpha Books
Author: Barbara Weltman
ISBN: 159257-333-9

Small Business Online
A Strategic Guide for Canada Entrepreneurs
Published by Prentice Hall Canada Inc.
Author: Jim Carroll with Rich Broadhead
ISBN: 0-13-976895-5

101 Ways To Promote your Website
Published by Maximum Press

Author: Susan Sweeney
ISBN: 1931644217

Start Your Own Business On eBay: Your Step by Step Guide To Success
Published by Entrepreneur Press
Author: Jacquelyn Lynn
ISBN: 1932531122

Start Your Own E-Business
Published by Entrepreneur Press
Author: Entrepreneur Press
ISBN: 1932156747

Selling On The Net: The Complete Guide
Published by NTC Business Books
Author: Lewis, Herschell Gordon
ISBN: 0844232343

Selling On The Internet: How To Open An Electronic Storefront And Have Millions Of Customers Come To You
Published by McGraw-Hill
Author: James C. Gonyea, Wayne M. Gonyea
ISBN: 0070241872

The Online Business Book
Published by Adam Media Corporation
Author: Rob Liflander
ISBN: 158062-3204

Guerrilla Marketing Online
Published by Houghton Mifflin
Author: Jay Conrad Levinson and Charles Rubin
ISBN: 0-395-86061-X

Internet Marketing For Dummies
Published by Wiley Publishing Inc.,
ISBN: 0-7645-0778-8

Low-Cost Website Promotion
Published by Adam Media Corporation
Author: Barry Feig
ISBN: 1-58062-501-0

Online Business Resources
Published by Made E-Z
Author: Paul Galloway

ISBN: 1-56382-510-4

Generating Trust in Online Business: From Theory To Practice
Published by IQ
Author: Magda Fusaro
ISBN: 2-922417-28-X

Absolute Beginners Guide to Launching an eBay Business
Published by Que
Author: Micheal Miller
ISBN: 0-7897-3058-8

Starting an eBay Business For Dummies
Published by Wiley Publishing Inc.,
Author: Marsha Collier
ISBN: 0-7645-6924-4

Online Business Planning
Published by Career Press
Author: Robert T. Gorman
ISBN: 1-56414-369-4

Marketing Without Advertising
Author: Michael Phillips, Salli Rasberry
ISBN: 0873376080

Guerrilla Publicity
Published by Adams Media Corporation
Author: Jay Conrad Levinson, Rich Frishman, Jill Lublin
ISBN: 1-58062-682-3

Marketing/How to get business
- Promote your website to increase the number of visitors
- Advertise in the yellow pages, newspapers, magazines and or billboards
- Brochures and flyers
- Business cards

Good luck!

Chapter 21

MASSAGE THERAPY

No ailment afflicts the human community as much as Pain, Aches, Anxiety and Stress. They have been around as long as mankind, and so has the endeavour of treating, curing and or managing them - Relaxation/Touch Therapy.

The oldest known documented historical evidence of massage therapy dates as far back as 3000BC. The first school of massage therapy sprung up in China in the early AD's. In 1895, Sigmund Freud used massage therapy to treat hysteria and in 1991, the Touch Research Institute was established. In 1992, Registration, Certification and Licensing became an issue for the massage therapy profession/trade. The Massage Registration Act was enacted in 1949 and the First Massage Act was passed in 1943 in the USA. North American students who came back from Europe where they went to study, introduced massage therapy in North America in the 1850's. The history of this profession/trade is so vast that people have been sent to jail for using Touch Therapy, as in the case of William Reich - an Austrian Psychoanalyst and one time student of Sigmund Freud. Mr Reich used the Somato Technique massage therapy in his attempt to cure Neuroses.

There are various forms of Massage Therapy, including:
Acupressure, Aromatherapy massage, Ayurvedic massage, Berry Work massage, Breast massage, Bowen therapy, Chi Nei Tsang massage, Equine massage, Esalen massage, Connective Tissue massage, Geriatric massage, Hawaiian massage, Hermopathy massage, Hot Stone massage, Infant massage, Iridiology massage, Medical massage, Myofascial release, Myotherapy massage, Naprapathy massage, Neuromuscular therapy, Chair massage, Orthopaedic massage, Pregnancy massage, Radiance Breathwork, Radiance Technique, Reflexology, Rosen method, Shiatsu massage, Soft Tissue Release massage, Sports massage, Swedish massage, Thai massage, Therapeutic Touch, Visceral Manipulation, Zero Balancing massage.

You can choose from any of these fields/types of massage to establish your practice/ business.

What You need To Start-Up

- A Computer (with Internet connection)

se a desktop or a laptop computer with a 56k modem. Install the following software on the computer:

- o **Word processor (MS Office) -** Use this to write letters, create mailing labels, and address envelopes. In the MS Office you've got MS Word, Excel, Access, Outlook, and PowerPoint.
- o **Spreadsheet** - You can create charts and do your finances with a spreadsheet program. Use MS Excel for your spreadsheet needs.
- o **QuickBooks Pro** - With this, you can create custom invoices, compute sales, do electronic banking, pay your bills, control your inventory and payroll. Use it for all accounting and bookkeeping.
- o **Database** - Use a database program to keep records of clients, sellers, vendors and all your business contacts/links. With the database program, you can keep records of phone calls, faxes, meetings, conferences and seminars, and note time and dates of events and incidents. You may want to use MS Access, Dbase or Fox Pro for your database needs.
- o **Graphic** - Use this to create flyers, announcements newsletters and advertisements. You may want to use PageMaker, QuarkXpress and ClarisWorks for your graphic exploits.
- o **Scheduler** - Use this to manage your schedules.
- Phone, Fax, Printer, Scanner, Copier (can buy all-in-one)
- Office Furniture (including office supplies and office accessories)
- Insurance
- Fees payable to become a member in professional and or trade associations.
- Books
- Marketing/advertising cost.

You will need some professional massage supply materials that may include:
Massage tables, Table accessories, Table packages, Massage chairs, Massage Oils, Lotions, Creams, Essential oils, Books, Massage charts, Activetics, Sheets and linens, Massage mats, T-shirts, Cold and hot packs, Massage tools, Anatomical chairs, Skeleton models, Body cushions, Cleaners, Hydrocollator, Paraffin bath, Videos and DVDs, Music, Pilates, Yoga supplies.

The occupation specific materials mentioned above could be gotten from:

Massage Therapy Supply Outlet
#203, 8815-92 Street
Edmonton, Alberta
T6C 3P9
Phone: 780-440-1818
Toll Free: 1-800-875-9706
Fax: 780-440-4585
Website: www.mtso.ab.ca

Or visit the following websites:
- www.accupunctureshop.com
- www.bodyworkmall.com
- www.promedproducts.com
- www.massagewarehouse.com
- www.sitincomfort.com
- www.stronglite.com
- www.massageproducts.com
- www.mohawkmedicalmall.com
- www.chinow.com
- www.massage-table-direct.com
- www.totalbodywork.com
- www.massage-chairs-direct.com
- www.aromanotes.com

The total cost of your start-up need may not exceed $20,000.

Professional/Trade Associations or Organizations you may need to join/know:

Canadian Massage Therapist Alliance (CMTA)
344 Lakeshore Road East, Suite B
Oakville, On
L6J 1J6
Phone: 905-849-7606
Fax: 905-849-8606
Email: info@cmta.ca
Website: www.cmta.ca

Massage Therapists Association of Alberta
Box 2403, RPO Plaza Centre
Red Deer, Alberta
T4N 6X6
Phone: 403-340-1913
Fax: 403-346-2269
Email: mtaa@telusplanet.net
Website: www.mtaaberta.com

Massage Therapists' Association of British Columbia (MTABC)
#205 - 640 West Broadway
Vancouver, British Columbia
V5V 1G4
Email: mta@smart.com
Website: www.massagetherapy.bc.ca

Massage Therapy Association of Manitoba, Inc. (NTAM)
BOX 65026 Elmwood,

355 Henderson Highway
Winnipeg MB
R2L 1MO
Phone: 204-254-0406
Fax: 204-661-1230
Email: mtam01@shaw.ca
Website: www.mtam.mb.ca

New Brunswick Massotherapy Association (NBMA)
P.O.BOX 20071
Fredericton NB
E3B 6Y8
Phone: 506-459-5788
Fax: 506-459-5581
Website: www.nbma-amnb.ca

Massage Therapists' Association of Nova Scotia (MTANS)
P.O.BOX 33103, Quinpool Post Office
Halifax, Nova Scotia
B3L 4T6
Phone: 902-429-2190

East Coast Massage Therapists Association Of Nova Scotia
Website: www.eastmassage.org

Ontario Massage Therapist Association (OMTA)
365 Bloor Street East, Suite 1807
Toronto, Ontario
M4W 3L4
Phone: 416-968-648Toll Free: 1-800-668-2022
Fax: 416-968-6818
Email: omta@colliscan.com

Prince Edwards Island Massage Therapy Association (PEIMTA)
P.O.BOX 1882
Charlottetown, PE
C1A 7N5
Phone: 902-368-8140
Fax: 902-368-6524

Federation Quebecoise Des Massotherapeutes (FQM)
1265, Mont-Royal est, bureau 204
Montreal, QC
H2J 1Y4
Phone: 514-597-0505

Toll Free: 1-800-363-9609
Fax: 514-597-0141
Email: administration@fqm.qc.ca
Website: www.fqm.qc.ca

Massage Therapist Association of Saskatchewan (MTAS)
230 Ave, R south, Room 327, Old Nurses Residence
Saskatoon, SK
S7M 0Z9
Phone: 306-384-7077
Fax: 306-384-7175
Email: mtas@sasktel.net

Canadian Sport Massage Therapists Association (CSMTA)
National Office at
1849 Yonge Street, Suite 814
Toronto, Ontario
M4S 1Y2
Phone: 416-488-4414
Fax: 416-488-3079
Email: natoffice@csmta.ca
Website: www.csmta.ca

The sport association has provincial offices in:
- **Ontario** - www.csmta.ca/on
- **Alberta** - www.csmta.ca/alberta
- **British Columbia** - www.csmta.ca/bc
- **Saskatchewan** - www.csmta.ca/sask

Books you may Need to Buy:

Building Your Ideal Private Practice: A Guide for Therapists and other Healing Professionals
Author: Lynn Grodzki
ISBN: 0393703312

Business Mastery: A Guide for Creating a Fulfilling, Thriving Business and Keeping it Successful.
Author: Cherie Sohnen-Moe
ISBN: 0962126543

Hands Heal: Communication, Documentation and Insurance Billing for Manual Therapists
Author: Diana L. Thompson
ISBN: 0781726824

Educated Heart: Professional Guidelines for Massage Therapists, Bodyworkers and Movement Teachers
Author: Nina M. McIntosh
ISBN: 096741220X

Myofascial & Deep Tissue Massage
Author: Alfred Hartemink

Deep Tissue massage: A Visual Guide To Techniques
Author: Art Riggs

Deep Tissue Massage and Myofascial Release: A Video Guide To Techniques
Author: Art Riggs

The Massage Connection: Anatomy and Physiology
Author: Kalyani Premkumar

Mosby's Pathology for Massage Therapists
Author: Susan G. Salvo

Pathology A to Z: A Handbook for Massage Therapists
Author: Kalyani Preskumar

Mosby's Fundamentals of Therapeutic Massage
Author: Sandy Fritz

Basic Clinical Massage Therapy: Integrating Anatomy and Treatment
Author: James H. Clay

A Massage Therapist's Guide to Pathology
Author: Ruth Werner

Trial Guide to the Body: How to Locate Muscles, Bones & More
Author: Andrew R. Biel

The Anatomy Coloring Book
Author: Wynn Kapit

Know How to Strengthen, Stretch and Make Your Body Flexible
Author: Alexis Wright

Review for Therapeutic Massage and Bodywork Certification
Author: Joseph Ashton

Have A Look At the Alternative World
Author: Gregg Strand

Guerrilla Publicity
Published by Adams Media Corporation
Author: Jay Conrad Levinson, Rich Frishman, Jill Lublin
ISBN: 1-58062-682-3

Marketing Without Advertising
Author: Michael Phillips, Salli Rasberry
ISBN: 0873376080

Endless Referrals: Network Your Everyday Contacts into Sales (New and Updated Edition)
Author: Bob Burg
ISBN: 0070089973

Marketing/How To Get Business

Hunting for business for your Massage Therapy Business Firm is about the same as searching for a job in your field. As such, you have to apply all the job search skills you have learnt over the years, customizing them to suit your present need and position.

- Cold calls to Health Clinics, Health Spas, Hospitals, Nursing Homes, Rehabilitation Centres, Companies, Businesses and Offices for information and interviews about who may need the services, and to provide them with reasons why they may need the services of your Massage Therapy Firm.
- Networking
- Yellow Pages advertisement
- Brochure/Flyers
- Business Cards
- Create a Website
- Join Associations/Social Clubs
- Distribute gift certificates and discounted treatment packages to your clients, to give to their friends
- Send out massage therapy package offers for special days and seasons like Christmas, New Year, Easter, Canada Day, Valentine's day, etc.
- or use your services for some time to remind them of your good service and new discount offers available.
- Find out and incorporate the marketing methods and approaches of other professionals in your field into your own method and approach.
- Call your clients, new/old/regular, a day or two after they use your services to thank them for using the services of your firm, but above all, to ask them how they are feeling.
- Offer discounts to your regular clients and offer them one free treatment session if they bring in four or more new clients.
- Send out a discounted Massage package for students, seniors, couples, singles, teenagers, and some specific professionals like lawyers, truck drivers, factory workers, teachers, etc.

- Massage of all forms and types helps to reduce stress and increase circulation. Develop a weekly newsletter, or write in the local newspaper and or magazine, giving tips on how to manage stress and use massage to increase circulation. Act like the professional you are.

Good luck!

Chapter 22

PACKAGING

Packaging is the act of assembling, wrapping and encasing a product, making it look more attractive and or portable than it is, for the sole purpose of selling it. The field of packaging is very wide. You can package anything, including water, sand and compost.

Food and Beverage Packaging: Biscuits, Cookies, Cereals, Confection, Dairy products, Dried food, Fresh and Frozen foods, Grocery products, Beverages, Juices, Cooking Oil, Nuts, Tea, Coffee, Soft drinks, Pet food, etc.

Pharmaceutical Packaging: Healthcare Packaging

Beauty, Personal Care and Cosmetic Products Packaging:
There is an amazing range of products to be packaged in this section including skin care, body care, hair care, toiletries, make-up and accessories – applicators, brushes, fragrances, perfumes, hair care etc. The demand for the products is increasing every day, and the consumer base is equally increasing.

- Science Products
- Industrial chemicals
- Lubricants
- Clothing Products
- Houseware
- Hardware
- Automotive Care Products
- Stationary
- Tobacco
- Information
- ETC

You may choose to buy products in bulk and repackage them to a chosen size and form, label them with your own brand name and sell them.

In this type of Packaging business, you need to:
- Identify/know a product you want to sell
- Find a manufacturer/bulk distributor
- Find a contract packaging company
- Determine your brand name
- Determine the form of packaging
- Selling Outlets – shops, stores, offices, etc.
- Obtain provincial licenses where applicable

Forms of Packaging:
Bags, Bottles, Boxes, Bundle wraps, Cans, Cases, Jars, Laminating, Moulds, Plastics, Tins, Tubes, Sachets, Soft packs, Wrapping, etc.

Depending on the type of product you decide to be packaging, you need to read the consumer packaging and labeling act, which outlines the rules and guidelines governing the packaging, labeling, sale, import and advertising of prepackaged products.
Consumer Packaging and Labeling Act (R.S. 1985, c. C-38)

What You need To Start-Up

- A Computer (with Internet connection)

  Use a desktop or a laptop computer with a 56k modem. Install the following software on the computer:
  - **Word processor (MS Office) -** Use this to write letters, create mailing labels, and address envelopes. In the MS Office you've got MS Word, Excel, Access, Outlook, and PowerPoint.
  - **Spreadsheet** - You can create charts and do your finances with a spreadsheet program. Use MS Excel for your spreadsheet needs.
  - **QuickBooks Pro** - With this, you can create custom invoices, compute sales, do electronic banking, pay your bills, control your inventory and payroll. Use it for all accounting and bookkeeping.
  - **Database** - Use a database program to keep records of clients, sellers, vendors and all your business contacts/links. With the database program, you can keep records of phone calls, faxes, meetings, conferences and seminars, and note time and dates of events and incidents. You may want to use MS Access, Dbase or Fox Pro for your database needs.
  - **Graphic** - Use this to create flyers, announcements newsletters and advertisements. You may want to use PageMaker, QuarkXpress and ClarisWorks for your graphic exploits.
  - **Scheduler** - Use this to manage your schedules.
- Phone, Fax, Printer, Scanner, Copier (can buy all-in-one)
- Office Furniture (including office supplies and office accessories)
- Insurance
- Fees payable to become a member in professional and or trade associations.

- Books
- Marketing/advertising cost.

Professional/Trade Associations You May Like To Join/Know:

Packaging Association of Canada - PAC
PAC is an Umbrella association with Chapters in Ontario, Alberta, Quebec, British Columbia, and the Prairies.

The Packaging Association of Canada
2255 Sheppard Avenue East
Suite E420
Toronto, ON
M2J 4Y1
Phone: 416-490-7860
Fax: 416 490-7844
Email: info@pac.ca

Bureau du Quebec
C.P. 43010
1859 René-Laennec
Succ. Vilamont
Laval, Québec
H7M 6A1
Phone: 514-990-0134
Fax: 450 668-2691
Email: quebec@pac.ca

Winnipeg
200 Omands Creek Boulevard
Winnipeg, MB
R2R 1V7
Tel: (204) 786-6873
Fax: (204) 786-1927

Atlantic
1176 Milne Avenue
New Minas, NS
B4N 4C8
Tel: (902) 681-0330
Fax: (902) 681-1629

Ottawa
Toll Free: 1-866-847-7107

Vancouver
600 Chester Road
Annacis Business Park
Delta, British Columbia
V3M 5Y3
Tel: (604) 515-3861
Fax: (604) 526-0788

Calgary
19 Lott Creek Hollow
Calgary, Alberta
T3Z 3A9
Tel: (403) 271-5390
Fax: (403) 217-0682

Canadian Importers Association
438 University Avenue
Suite 1618
P.O.BOX 60
Toronto, Ontario
M5G 2K8
Phone: 416-595-5333
Website: www.importers.ca
This Association offers seminars for their new members - 'Import Canada'

The Alliance of Manufacturers and Exporters Canada
1 Nicholas Street,
Suite 1500
Ottawa, Ontario
K1N 7B7
Phone: 613-238-8888
Website: www.the-alliance.org

5995 Avesbury Road
Suite 900
Mississauga Ontario
L5R 3P9
Phone: 905-568-8300

75 International Boulevard,
Suite 400
Toronto, Ontario
M9W 6L9
Phone: 416-798-8000
Fax: 416-798-8050

Books You May Need To Buy:

Packaging Source Book (Hardcover)
By Robert Opie
Publisher: Book Sales (November, 1991)
ISBN: 1555215114

Package Design: An Introduction to the Art of Packaging (A Spectrum book)
By Laslo Roth
Publisher: Prentice Hall (January 1, 1981)
ISBN: 0136478425

How To Be Your Own Publicist
Published by McGraw-Hill
Author: Jessica Hatchigan
ISBN:0-07-138332-8

6 Steps To Free Publicity
Published by Career Press Inc.
Author: Marcia Yudkin
ISBN: 1-56414-675-8

Selling Through Independent Representatives
Published by AMACON
Author: Harold J. Novick
ISBN: 0-8144-0522-3

Thomas Register of Manufacturers
Website: www.thomasregister.com

The Export Directory of Canada
Contains a List of Canadian Manufacturers, Procedures and Exports

A list of Manufacturing Firms in British Columbia
Organized by size, grouped according to employment
Published by Victoria British Columbia
Author: BC Bureau of Economics and Statistics

Your Guide to Statistics Canada's New Census of Manufacturers Publication

Selling to Government
A Guide to Government Procurement in Canada

Multinational Distribution Channel
Tax and Legal Strategies
Author: R. Dudane Hall, Ralph J. Gilbert

ISBN: 0275901157

Successful Cold Call Selling
Published by American Management Association
Author: Lee Boyan
ISBN: 0-8144-7718-6

Guerrilla Publicity
Published by Adams Media Corporation
Author: Jay Conrad Levinson, Rich Frishman and Jill Lublin
ISBN: 1-58062-682-3

Marketing Without Advertising
Author: Michael Phillips, Salli Rasberry
ISBN: 0873376080

Other sources of information include:
- Seminars
- Magazines
- Journals
- Newsletters
- Trade Publications
- Websites

Marketing/How To Get Business
Hunting for business for your Consumer Packaging firm is about the same as searching for a job, you have to apply all the job search skills you have acquired over the years, customizing them to suit your present need and position.
- Cold calls to Manufacturers, Companies, Businesses, Offices, and Organizations for information and interviews about who wants what, and to provide them with your profile.
- Make contact with the trade division of Embassies and Consulates of foreign countries for product leads in their countries.
- Visit Chambers of Commerce
- Networking
- Brochures/Flyers
- Business Cards
- Create a Website
- Join Associations/Social Clubs
- Trade Fairs

Good luck!

Chapter 23

PRODUCING HOW-TO VIDEOS AND DVDS

Nowadays, there are how-to books in almost every topic. Likewise there are how-to-videos on almost everything, and it takes less time to produce how to videos than how-to books, and both sells equally. You only need to tell the story with a camera rather than a pen and paper. How-to videos are also easier for the consumer to use. The consumer needs between 45 minutes and 90 minutes to see and hear the how-to lesson. The single factor that drives the sales of how-to-videos is the topic. You can start off producing how-to videos with the equipment you already have – a camcorder and a computer.

However, to produce how-to videos and DVDs, you need basic knowledge of:
- Marketable topics
- Script writing
- Camcorder/Video shooting techniques
- Computerized video editing
- Setting up a home/office video studio
- How to add graphics, titles and background audio to video
- Lighting techniques
- How to create video graphics
- The use of chromakey backgrounds
- Correct video equipment
- Converting the video to a DVD
- Recording sound
- Shooting a conversation
- There are various types of videos you can produce including:
- Seduction
- Corporate videos
- Legal education
- Educational videos
- Manufacturing
- Computer programs
- Architecture
- Waterfront construction
- Swimming Pool Construction

- Etc.

What You need To Start-Up

- A Computer (with Internet connection)

    Use a desktop or a laptop computer with a 56k modem. Install the following software on the computer:
    - **Word processor (MS Office) -** Use this to write letters, create mailing labels, and address envelopes. In the MS Office you've got MS Word, Excel, Access, Outlook, and PowerPoint.
    - **Spreadsheet** - You can create charts and do your finances with a spreadsheet program. Use MS Excel for your spreadsheet needs.
    - **QuickBooks Pro** - With this, you can create custom invoices, compute sales, do electronic banking, pay your bills, control your inventory and payroll. Use it for all accounting and bookkeeping.
    - **Database** - Use a database program to keep records of clients, sellers, vendors and all your business contacts/links. With the database program, you can keep records of phone calls, faxes, meetings, conferences and seminars, and note time and dates of events and incidents. You may want to use MS Access, Dbase or Fox Pro for your database needs.
    - **Graphic** - Use this to create flyers, announcements newsletters and advertisements. You may want to use PageMaker, QuarkXpress and ClarisWorks for your graphic exploits.
    - **Scheduler** - Use this to manage your schedules.
- Phone, Fax, Printer, Scanner, Copier (can buy all-in-one)
- Office Furniture (including office supplies and office accessories)
- Video camera
- DVD writer
- Insurance
- Fees payable to become a member in professional and or trade associations.
- Books
- Marketing/advertising cost.

Books You May Need To Buy:

Writing, Directing, and Producing Documentary Films and Videos
By Alan Rosenthal
Publisher: Southern Illinois University Press
ISBN: 0809324482

Making Documentary Films and Reality Videos: A Practical Guide to Planning, Filming, and Editing documentaries of Real Events
By Barry Hampe

Documentary Storytelling for Video and Filmmakers
By Sheila Curran Bernard

Directing the Documentary, Fourth Edition
By Michael Rabiger

Introduction to Documentary
By Bill Nicholas

Documentary Filmmakers Speak
By Liz Stubbs

Digital Filmmaking 101: An Essential Guide to producing Low Budget Movies
By Dale Newton

Rebel Without a Crew: Or How a 23-Year-Old Filmmaker Became a Hollywood Player
By Robert Rodriguez

Shaking the Money Tree, 2nd Edition: How to Get grants and Donations for Film and Video
By Morrie Warshawski

Lighting for Digital Video & Television, Second Edition
By John Jackman

Documentary: A History of the Non-Fiction Film
By Erik Barnouw

Guerrilla Publicity
Published by Adams Media Corporation
Author: Jay Conrad Levinson, Rich Frishman, Jill Lublin
ISBN: 1-58062-682-3

Marketing Without Advertising
Author: Michael Phillips, Salli Rasberry
ISBN: 0873376080

The 22 Immutable Laws of Marketing
Published by Harper Business
Author: Al Ries and Jack Trout
ISBN: 0887306667

6 Steps To Free Publicity
Published by Career Press Inc
Author: Marcia Yudkin
ISBN: 1-56414-675-8

How To Become Your Own Publicist
Published by McGraw-Hill
Author: Jessica Hatchigan
ISBN:0-07-138332-8

Endless Referrals: Network Your Everyday Contacts into Sales (New and Updated Edition)
Author: Bob Burg
ISBN: 0070089973

Marketing/How To Get Business

- First of all, you must produce videos and DVDs on topics that sell.
- Networking
- Brochures/Flyers
- Business Cards
- Create a Website
- Trade Fairs

Chapter 24

RESEARCH AND INFORMATION BROKER/ PROFESSIONAL

Information is the strategic resource with which companies, businesses, organizations, professionals, and people work. Better access to information has led to increased productivity, better service and general efficiency, as well as more direct approach to problems and difficulties. Many companies, businesses, organizations, professionals and individuals are employing the services of research and information brokers/ professionals to track down information they may need to increase productivity, improve service and general efficiency in the workplace, to resolve a specific problem, to stage viable competition, to elaborate an idea, to vet an innovation, etc.

Various names have been employed by the public in an attempt to describe this profession - names like information retriever, information merchant, information finder, information expert, information agent, information researcher, desktop Internet researcher, information professional and information broker. No matter what name someone chooses to call the trade, it all points to trading on information - to chasing down and retrieving specific information for a price.

As a Research and Information Broker/Professional, you will be in the business of chasing down and retrieving specific information as desired by your client. Your clients may include Companies, Businesses, Banks, Organizations, Professionals and Individuals. The information your clients want may range from historical, social, public records, commercial, sports, literary, legal, to scientific, technological, architecture, medical, financial and abstract information. For quicker and easier access to information, you may need to subscribe to online databases.

As a Research and Information Broker/Professional, you need to:
- Be research oriented
- Be curious
- Have interviewing skills
- Be able to use the library extensively
- Pay attention to detail
- Be analytical
- Be able to meet deadlines
- Be able to use questioning and interviewing to develop leads

As a professional and or skilled person, you may like to specialize in your field and areas related to your field of expertise.

What You need To Start-Up

- A Computer (with Internet connection)

  Use a desktop or a laptop computer with a 56k modem. Install the following software on the computer:
  - o **Word processor (MS Office)** - Use this to write letters, create mailing labels, and address envelopes. In the MS Office you've got MS Word, Excel, Access, Outlook, and PowerPoint.
  - o **Spreadsheet** - You can create charts and do your finances with a spreadsheet program. Use MS Excel for your spreadsheet needs.
  - o **QuickBooks Pro** - With this, you can create custom invoices, compute sales, do electronic banking, pay your bills, control your inventory and payroll. Use it for all accounting and bookkeeping.
  - o **Database** - Use a database program to keep records of clients, sellers, vendors and all your business contacts/links. With the database program, you can keep records of phone calls, faxes, meetings, conferences and seminars, and note time and dates of events and incidents. You may want to use MS Access, Dbase or Fox Pro for your database needs.
  - o **Graphic** - Use this to create flyers, announcements newsletters and advertisements. You may want to use PageMaker, QuarkXpress and ClarisWorks for your graphic exploits.
  - o **Scheduler** - Use this to manage your schedules.
- Phone, Fax, Printer, Scanner, Copier (can buy all-in-one)
- Office Furniture (including office supplies and office accessories)
- Insurance
- Fees payable to become a member in professional and or trade associations.
- Books
- Marketing/advertising cost.
- Business suits, ties, shoes, briefcase (all for personal image improvement) and other miscellaneous expenses

The total cost of your start-up needs will not exceed $20,000 Canadian.

Books You May Need to Buy:

Building and Running a Successful Research Business: A Guide for The Independent Information Professional
Author: Mary Ellen Bates

Find IT Online: The Complete Guide To Online Research (Third Edition)
Author: Alan M. Schlein

The Invisible Web: Uncovering Information Sources Search Engines Can't See
Author: Chris Sherman

Super Searchers Make It On Their Own: Top Independent Information Professionals Share their Secrets For Starting and Running A Research Business
Author: Suzanne Sabroski

Find It Fast: How to Uncover Expert Information on Any Subject
Author: Robert I. Berkman

Naked in Cyberspace: How To Find Personal Information Online
Author: Carole A. Lane, Helen Burwell, Hellen P. Burwell, Owen Davies

Researching Public Records: How To Get Anything on Anybody
Author: Vincent Parco

The Online 100: Online Magazines Field Guide To The 100 Most Important Online Databases
Published by Cyberage Books
Author: Mick O'Leary
ISBN: 0910965145

Information Brokering: A How-To-Do-It Manual (How-To-Do-It Manual for Libraries, No 86)
Author: Florence Mason

Super Searchers Go To The Source: The Interviewing and Hands-on Information Strategies For Primary Researchers-Online, on the Phone, and in Person (Super Searchers, V.7)
Author: Risa Sacks

The Extreme Searcher's Internet Handbook: A Guide for the Serious Searcher
Author: Gary Price

Super Searchers on Competitive Intelligence: The Online and Offline Secrets of Top CI Researchers
Author: Jan Herring

Encyclopaedia of Investigative Information Sources
Author: J. Michael Ball

Researching Online for Dummies
Published by IDG Books
Author: Reva Basch
ISBN: 0764503820

The Online Deskbook: Online Magazine's Essential Desk Reference for online and Internet Searchers
Published by Independent Publishing Group
Author: Mary Ellen Bates and Reva Basch
ISBN: 0910965196

The Investigators Little Black Book 2
Author: Robert Scott

The Information Brokers Handbook
Published by McGraw-Hill
Author: Sue Rugge and Alfred Glossbrenner
ISBN: 0070578710

Find Public Records Fast: The Complete State, County and Courthouse Locator
Published by Facts on Demand Press
ISBN: 1889150045

Start Your Own Information Consultant Business
Published by Entrepreneur Media
Author: Walsh George
ISBN: 1932156739

Guerrilla Publicity
Published by Adams Media Corporation
Author: Jay Conrad Levinson, Rich Frishman, Jill Lublin
ISBN: 1-58062-682-3

Marketing Without Advertising
Author: Michael Phillips, Salli Rasberry
ISBN: 0873376080

The 22 Immutable Laws of Marketing
Published by Harper Business
Author: Al Ries and Jack Trout
ISBN: 0887306667

6 Steps To Free Publicity
Published by Career Press Inc
Author: Marcia Yudkin
ISBN: 1-56414-675-8

How To Become Your Own Publicist
Published by McGraw-Hill
Author: Jessica Hatchigan
ISBN:0-07-138332-8

Endless Referrals: Network Your Everyday Contacts into Sales (New and Updated Edition)
Author: Bob Burg
ISBN: 0070089973

Marketing/How To Get Business

Hunting for business for your Information Brokerage firm is about the same as searching for a job in your field. As such, you have to apply all the job search skills you have learnt over the years, customizing them to suit your present need and position.

- Cold calls to Manufacturers, Companies, Businesses, Offices, and Organizations for information interviews about who wants what information, and to provide them with your profile.
- Make contact with the trade division of Embassies and Consulates of foreign countries for information brokerage leads in their countries.
- Visit Chambers of Commerce
- Networking
- Brochures/Flyers
- Business Cards
- Create a Website
- Join Associations/Social Clubs
- Trade Fairs

Good luck!

Chapter 25
HEADHUNTER/EXECUTIVE RECRUITER

Did you ever employ the services of a headhunting firm in your endeavour to secure an employment opportunity in your field of expertise/interest, before you braved up and said goodbye to job search and to paid employment, and chose to buy yourself a job by becoming self-employed and owning your own business?

Yes?

No?

Well, whatever your response is, it is always interesting to watch a scene where the beggar, for whatever reason rises to become the giver. By choosing headhunting as a business, not only do you own your business, become your own boss and take control of your financial and professional being, you also rise to give to others what you may have asked for, but did not receive.

Headhunting is the business of employment brokerage. As a headhunter, you match job seeking qualified professionals and or skilled persons with employers and employment opportunities. You will be tracking down specific talents/professionals as desired by your clients, for a price. You are essentially a matchmaker. Your clients may include Companies, Businesses, Organizations, Governments, offices, other professionals, and Individuals.

Up to two-thirds of hiring in Canada is done through networking. Companies often ask their employees for help in filling a job vacancy in the company. Companies also turn to Headhunters for help. The reasons include:

- It is far cheaper for the companies to use Headhunters and or the effort of their employees to fill vacancy, than to pay for advertisement in the newspaper.
- It saves the Human Resources Department the time of going through heaps of resumes from job seekers.
- The prospective employee will have a reference known to the company/ employer.

When a Headhunter fills a job vacancy for an employer, the employer pays the Headhunter a certain percentage of the employee's agreed monthly or annual wage - an amount of money that may equal the employee's wage for one-week, two weeks, one-month, two months or one year, depending on the contract. But this amount is not deducted from the employee's wage. A headhunter may not bargain for an employee's wage, but may communicate the employees wage expectations to the employer. Headhunters may offer a guarantee of three months, six months, one year depending on the nature of the job and or the contract. If the employee, for any reason doesn't stay for the period covered in the guarantee, the Headhunter makes a replacement at no extra cost to the employer.

You may choose to specialize in a particular Industry, Field, Trade, and or Profession. As a professional, you may choose to specialize in your own field of expertise. This gives you an edge because you know the field, the profession, and the needed skills. As such, you will be able to vet the quality/calibre of professionals you will be sending to your clients and vice versa.

As a Headhunter, you need to:
- Be People Smart
- Be Trendy
- Be Pro-active
- Be analytical
- Be able to meet deadlines
- Maintain a list of clients
- Have knowledge of the company(s) to which you send your clients
- Know the job description
- Have marketing/advertising skills
- Have interviewing skills
- Have a Matchmaker's instinct
- Be research oriented

What You need To Start-Up

- A Computer (with Internet connection)

  Use a desktop or a laptop computer with a 56k modem. Install the following software on the computer:
  - **Word processor (MS Office)** - Use this to write letters, create mailing labels, and address envelopes. In the MS Office you've got MS Word, Excel, Access, Outlook, and PowerPoint.
  - **Spreadsheet** - You can create charts and do your finances with a spreadsheet program. Use MS Excel for your spreadsheet needs.
  - **QuickBooks Pro** - With this, you can create custom invoices, compute sales, do electronic banking, pay your bills, control your inventory and payroll. Use it for all accounting and bookkeeping.
  - **Database** - Use a database program to keep records of clients, sellers, vendors and all your business contacts/links. With the database program, you can keep records of phone calls, faxes, meetings, conferences and seminars, and note time and dates of events and incidents. You may want to use MS Access, Dbase or Fox Pro for your database needs.
  - **Graphic** - Use this to create flyers, announcements newsletters and advertisements. You may want to use PageMaker, QuarkXpress and ClarisWorks for your graphic exploits.
  - **Scheduler** - Use this to manage your schedules.
- Phone, Fax, Printer, Scanner, Copier (can buy all-in-one)
- Office Furniture (including office supplies and office accessories)
- Insurance
- Fees payable to become a member in professional and or trade associations.
- Books
- Marketing/advertising cost.

- Business suits, ties, shoes, briefcase (all for personal image improvement) and other miscellaneous expenses

The total cost of your start-up needs will not exceed $20,000 Canadian.

Professional/Trade Associations You May Like To Join/Know:

Association of Professional Recruiters of Canada
Ste. 2210-1081 Ambleside Drive,
Ottawa, Ontario
K2B 8C8
Phone: 613-721-5957
Toll Free: 1-888-441-0000
Fax: 613-721-5850
Email: info@workplace.ca
Website: www.workplace.ca

Canadian Network of Recruiters, Headhunters, Executive Search Firms, Employment Agencies and Management Consultants
1200 Markham Road, Suite 107
Toronto, Ontario
M1H 3C3
Phone: 416-438-3606
Fax: 416-438-1849
Email: info@recruiterwebsites.com
Website: www.recruiterwebsites.com

National Association of Executive Search Recruiters

Books You May Need To Buy:

Headhunters: Matchmaking in The Labour Market
Published by ILR Press
Author: William Finlay, James E. Coverdill
ISBN: 0801439272

The Headhunter's Edge
Published by Random House
Author: Jefferey E. Christian
ISBN: 0375505431

Start Your Own Executive Recruiting Business
Published by Entrepreneur Press
Author: Entrepreneur Press, Erickson Mandy
ISBN: 189198490X

The Complete Guide to owning and operating a House-Based Recruiting Business: A Step-by-Step business Plan For Entrepreneurs
Published by Writers Club Press
Author: Charrissa D. Cawley
ISBN: 0595163955

How To Market and Sell Your Recruiting Services
Published by Innovative Consulting
Author: Bill Radin
ISBN: 1929836007

Advanced Strategies For Recruiters
Published by Innovative consulting
Author: Bill Radin
ISBN: 1929836104

The Recruiters Research Blue Book
Published by Kennedy information
Author: Andrea A. Jupina
ISBN: 1885922612

Recruiting on the Web: Smart Strategies For Finding The Perfect Candidate
Published by McGraw-Hill
Author: Michael Foster
ISBN: 0071384855

Effective Recruiting Strategies: Taking a Marketing Approach
Published by Crisp Publications
Author: Ron Visconti
ISBN: 1560521279

The Keys To Successful Recruiting and Staffing
Published by Weddle's
Author: Barry Siegel
ISBN: 1928734170

Guerrilla Publicity
Published by Adams Media Corporation
Author: Jay Conrad Levinson, Rich Frishman, Jill Lublin
ISBN: 1-58062-682-3

Marketing Without Advertising
Author: Michael Phillips, Salli Rasberry
ISBN: 0873376080

The 22 Immutable Laws of Marketing

Published by Harper Business
Author: Al Ries and Jack Trout
ISBN: 0887306667

6 Steps To Free Publicity
Published by Career Press Inc
Author: Marcia Yudkin
ISBN: 1-56414-675-8

How To Become Your Own Publicist
Published by McGraw-Hill
Author: Jessica Hatchigan
ISBN:0-07-138332-8

Endless Referrals: Network Your Everyday Contacts into Sales (New and Updated Edition)
Author: Bob Burg
ISBN: 0070089973

Marketing/How To Get Business

Hunting for business for your Headhunting firm is about the same as searching for a job in your field. As such, you have to apply all the job search skills you have acquired over the years, customizing them to suit your present need and position.
- Cold calls to Manufacturers, Companies, Businesses, Offices, and Organizations for information and interviews about who wants to employ a professional, and to provide them with your profile
- Advertise in the local/national newspapers, offering employment opportunities and job placements. Place another advertisement offering Businesses, Companies, Organizations, and Offices your help finding qualified professionals and skilled employees
- Find out and incorporate the marketing methods and approaches of other professionals in your field into your own method and approach
- Networking
- Brochures/Flyers
- Business Cards
- Create a Website
- Join Associations/Social Clubs
- Trade Fairs

Good luck!

Chapter 26

TOUR OPERATOR/TOURIST GUIDE

Tour Operation depends largely on environmental and cultural resources. As a tour operator, you must not only love travelling, sightseeing, culture and the environment, but you must have a good knowledge of memorable and pleasurable places and tourist sites.

According to the definition by the European Committee for Standardisation (CEN), a tourist guide is a person who guides visitors, speaking the language of their choice, to interpret the cultural and natural heritage of an area. This person normally possesses an area-specific qualification, usually issued and or recognised by the appropriate authority.

A tour manager is a person who manages the itinerary on behalf of the tour operator, ensuring the programme is carried out as described in the tour operator's literature, and sold to the traveller/consumer. A tour manager also gives practical local information.

As a tour operator/tourist guide, you must be conversant with the code of guiding practice adopted by the World Federation of Tourist Guides Association (WFTGA):
- Promote a professional service to visitors, be professional in care and commitment and professional in providing an objective understanding of the place(s) visited, free from prejudice or propaganda.
- Ensure that, as far as possible, what is presented as fact is true, and that a clear distinction is made between this truth and stories, legends, tradition or opinions.
- Act fairly and reasonably in dealing with all those who engage the services of guides, and with colleagues working in all aspects of tourism.
- Protect the reputation of tourism in the country by making every endeavour to ensure that guided groups treat, with respect, the environment, wildlife, sights and monuments, and also local customs and sensitivities.
- As representatives of the host country, to welcome visitors, and promote the country as a tourist destination.

The WFTGA aims to establish contact with tourist guide associations throughout the world, and to reinforce their professional ties. It strives to represent professional tourist guides internationally, and to promote and protect their interests. The association aims to enhance the image of the profession, and to promote a universal code of ethics and skills: to raise, encourage and establish the highest standards of professionalism. The WFTGA aims to develop international training and improving the quality of guiding through education.

When organizing a tour, you have to consider: environmental, social, and economic aspects. In general, tours can be organized around various interests, hobbies, sports or adventures, including: Picnicking, Mountain climbing, Cave exploration, Parachuting, Sea diving, Bicycle, Walking, River-rafting, Rock climbing, Kayaking, Cross country skiing, Downhill skiing, Skiing resorts, Golfing, Forests and Camping.

Tours can also be organized for special niche clients, such as: Seniors, Students, Couples, Children, Travelling families and Business executives, Sports teams and clubs.

You may choose to specialize on any of the different kinds of tours and clients.

For an effective tour operating business, you need tour operator's software. Some of these software systems cover the A to Z: all aspects of inbound and outbound tour operating business.
Visit the website: www.caterra.com/tour-operating-software
You will have a list of over 45 Tour Operating software packages.

What You need To Start-Up

- A Computer (with Internet connection)

  Use a desktop or a laptop computer with a 56k modem. Install the following software on the computer:
  - **Word processor (MS Office) -** Use this to write letters, create mailing labels, and address envelopes. In the MS Office you've got MS Word, Excel, Access, Outlook, and PowerPoint.
  - **Spreadsheet** - You can create charts and do your finances with a spreadsheet program. Use MS Excel for your spreadsheet needs.
  - **QuickBooks Pro** - With this, you can create custom invoices, compute sales, do electronic banking, pay your bills, control your inventory and payroll. Use it for all accounting and bookkeeping.
  - **Database** - Use a database program to keep records of clients, sellers, vendors and all your business contacts/links. With the database program, you can keep records of phone calls, faxes, meetings, conferences and seminars, and note time and dates of events and incidents. You may want to use MS Access, Dbase or Fox Pro for your database needs.
  - **Graphic** - Use this to create flyers, announcements newsletters and advertisements. You may want to use PageMaker, QuarkXpress and ClarisWorks for your graphic exploits.
  - **Scheduler** - Use this to manage your schedules.

- Phone, Fax, Printer, Scanner, Copier (can buy all-in-one)
- Office Furniture (including office supplies and office accessories)
- Insurance
- Tour Operator's Software
- Video Camera (Digital preferably)
- Photo Camera (Digital preferably)
- Fees payable to become a member in professional and or trade associations.
- Books
- Marketing/advertising cost.
- Business suits, ties, shoes, briefcase (all for personal image improvement) and other miscellaneous expenses

The total cost of your start-up needs will not exceed $20,000 Canadian.

Professional/Trade Associations You May Like To Join/Know:

World Federation of Tourist Guides Association Head Office
The WFTGA Administrator,
Wirtschaftskammer Wien
FG Freizeitbetriebe
Judenplats 3 - 4
1010 Wien
Austria
Phone: 43 1 51450 4211
Fax: 43 1 51450 4216
Email: info@wftga.org
Website: www.wftga.org

Representative of the Federation in Canada
Houri Nazaretian
1363 Wecker Drive
Oshawa, Ontario
L1J 3P8
Phone: 905-721-0783
Fax; 905-721-9062
Email; knazaretia@aol.com

Canadian Tour Guide Association of Toronto
122-250, The Eastmall, Suite 1705
Toronto, Ontario
M9B 6L3
Phone: 416-410-8621
Fax: 416-410-8621
Email; info@ctgaoftoronto.org
Website: www.ctgaoftoronto.org

Association des Guides Touristiques des Quebec Inc.
College Merici
Case Postale 79
755, Chemin St.-Louis
Quebec City, QC
G1S 1C1

The Alberta Tour Directors Association
Box 8044
Canmore, Alberta
T1W 2T8
Phone: 403-678-2833
Email: ctconsultants@monarc.net
Contact: Alison Day

Association Professionalle des Guides Touristiques
Chapitre de Montreal (APGT)
C.P. 982, Succursale Place d'Armes
Montreal, QC
H2Y 3J4
Phone: 514-990-9849
Email: renelemieuxguide@hotmail.com
Contact: Rene Lemieux
Website: www.apgtmontreal.org

Canadian tour Guides Association of British Columbia
BOX 2440
Vancouver, British Columbia
V6B 3W7
Phone: 604-876-2576
Fax: 604-872-2640
Email: jeff@ctgaofbc.com
Contact: Jeff Veniot
Website: www.ctgaofbc.com

Capital Tour Guide Association
496 Parkdale Ave.
Ottawa, Ontario
K1Y 0A3
Phone: 613-722-5939
Fax: 613-722-5743
Contact: Lenore Leon

Books you May Need to Buy
Conducting Tours: A Practical Guide
Published by Thomas Delmar learning

Author: Marc Mancini, Terri Gaylord
ISBN: 076681419X

Start Your Own Specialty Travel & Tour Business
Published by Self-Counsel Press
Author: Barbara Braidwood
ISBN: 1551802848

Successful International Tour Director: How To Become an International Tour Director
Published by Authors Choice Press
Author: Geralde Mitchell
ISBN: 0595167020

Internet Marketing For Your Tourism Business: Proven Techniques for Promoting Tourist Based Business Over The Internet
Published by Maximum Press
Author: Susan Sweeney
ISBN: 1885068476

Becoming A Tour Guide: The Principles of Guiding and Site Interpretation
Published by Int. Thomson Business Press
Author: Verite Reily Collins
ISBN: 0826447880

The Professional Guide: Dynamics of Tour Guiding
Published by Wiley
Author: Kathleen Lingle Pond
ISBN: 047128386X

Essentials of Tour Management
Published by Prentice hall
Author: Betsy Fay
ISBN: 0132850656

The Good Guide: A Sourcebook For Interpreters, Docents, And Tour Guides
Published by Ironwood Press
Author: Alison L. Grinder
ISBN: 0932541003

Selling Destinations: Geography For The Travel Professional
Published by Delmar Thompson Learning
Author: Marc Mancini
ISBN: 1401819826

How To Start A Home-Based Travel Agency
Published by Tom Ogg and Associates
Author: Tom Ogg
ISBN: 1888290056

Guerrilla Publicity
Published by Adams Media Corporation
Author: Jay Conrad Levinson, Rich Frishman, Jill Lublin
ISBN: 1-58062-682-3

Marketing Without Advertising
Author: Michael Phillips, Salli Rasberry
ISBN: 0873376080

The 22 Immutable Laws of Marketing
Published by Harper Business
Author: Al Ries and Jack Trout
ISBN: 0887306667

6 Steps To Free Publicity
Published by Career Press Inc.
Author: Marcia Yudkin
ISBN: 1-56414-675-8

Endless Referrals: Network Your Everyday Contacts into Sales (New and Updated Edition)
Author: Bob Burg
ISBN: 0070089973
How To Become Your Own Publicist
Published by McGraw-Hill
Author: Jessica Hatchigan
ISBN:0-07-138332-8

Marking/How To Get Business

Hunting for business for your Tour Operating/Management Firm is about the same as searching for a job in your field. As such, you have to apply all the job search skills you have learnt over the years, customizing them to suit your present need and position.
- Cold calls to Schools, Organizations and Conference/Convention Organizers for information and interviews about who may need the services, and to provide them with reasons they may need the services of your Tour Operating/ Management Firm.
- Network with other tour operators nationally and internationally. You can be exchanging tour packages, andsending and receiving tourist groups to and from countries around the globe.

- Yellow Pages advertisement
- Brochures/Flyers
- Business Cards
- Create a Website
- Join Associations/Social Clubs
- Distribute gift certificates and discounted tour packages to your clients to give to their friends
- Send out tour package offers for special days and seasons like Christmas, New Year, Easter, Canada Day, Valentine's Day, etc.
- Keep in touch with your clients and call the clients who have not used your services for sometime to remind them of your good services and new discount offers available.
- Find out and incorporate the marketing methods and approaches of other professionals in your field into your own method and approach.
- Call your clients - new/old/regular, a day or two after they use your services to thank them for using the services of your tour management firm, but above all, to ask them how they are feeling, and if they enjoyed the trip.
- Offer discounts to your regular clients and offer them free tour packages if they bring in four or more new clients - referral reward
- Send out a discounted tour package offer for students, seniors, couples, singles, teenagers, and some specific professions/professionals like lawyers, truck drivers, factory workers, teachers etc, including a lecture session on a particular topic.
- Develop a weekly newsletter, write in the local newspaper and or magazine giving tips on how to increase awareness, enrich ones cultural sense, love and promote the environment and cultural heritages, and use tour and sight seeing to manage stress. Act like the professional you are.

Good luck!

Chapter 27

PUBLIC RELATIONS PROFESSIONAL/PUBLICIST

A Public Relations Professional/Publicist is a person who is in the business of creating, generating and or drumming up publicity in the media for a client, the client's product(s) or the client's service(s), with the sole intention of improving the client's public image.

The clientele of a publicist may include celebrities - singers, sportsmen, actors, politicians, governments, businesses, industries, companies and organizations.

The Publicist stages a goodwill campaign for the client during their heydays and crisis period. In every campaign the publicist aims to earn a favourable public image/opinion for the client.

A publicist may choose to specialize in one or more of the various areas of specialization in the field of public relations, such as:
- Celebrity affairs
- Entertainment
- Government affairs
- Political affairs
- Organizations
- Public affairs
- Industry/Company/Business affairs
- Science/Technology/Research
- Crisis management/Damage control
- Racial/Multicultural affairs
- Fundraising/Charity
- Events
- Environmental affairs
- Private practice

At all times, the members of these specialized areas seek the services of the publicist to gain positive publicity. However, a publicist could be contacted to stage a negative campaign about a competitor on behalf of a client with the sole aim of generating negative publicity for the competitor.

As a publicist, you need to:
- Be persistent, persuasive, confident and diplomatic
- Have a craving for trends - the ability to read a lot and know the current trends (Trendy)
- Have contacts in the media (editors)
- Know the kind of story each editor/contact works with
- Have excellent communication skills
- Be people smart
- Have teamwork skills
- Have excellent telephone skills/manners
- Have excellent writing/report writing skills
- Be very creative - be able to package a story/report to make it as attractive and newsworthy as possible
- Have presentation skills
- Be able to meet deadlines
- Be very professional
- Have a craving for information - be addicted to the act of searching for information

You may choose to specialize in an area related to your field of expertise.

What You need To Start-Up

- A Computer (with Internet connection)

  Use a desktop or a laptop computer with a 56k modem. Install the following software on the computer:
  - **Word processor (MS Office)** - Use this to write letters, create mailing labels, and address envelopes. In the MS Office you've got MS Word, Excel, Access, Outlook, and PowerPoint.
  - **Spreadsheet** - You can create charts and do your finances with a spreadsheet program. Use MS Excel for your spreadsheet needs.
  - **QuickBooks Pro** - With this, you can create custom invoices, compute sales, do electronic banking, pay your bills, control your inventory and payroll. Use it for all accounting and bookkeeping.
  - **Database** - Use a database program to keep records of clients, sellers, vendors and all your business contacts/links. With the database program, you can keep records of phone calls, faxes, meetings, conferences and seminars, and note time and dates of events and incidents. You may want to use MS Access, Dbase or Fox Pro for your database needs.
  - **Graphic** - Use this to create flyers, announcements newsletters and advertisements. You may want to use PageMaker, QuarkXpress and ClarisWorks for your graphic exploits.
  - **Scheduler** - Use this to manage your schedules.
- Phone, Fax, Printer, Scanner, Copier (can buy all-in-one)

- Office Furniture (including office supplies and office accessories)
- Insurance
- Fees payable to become a member in professional and or trade associations.
- Books
- PR Software system
- Video Camera (preferably digital)
- Photo Camera (preferably digital)
- Audio Recorder (preferably digital)
- Marketing/advertising cost.
- Business suits, ties, shoes, briefcase (all for personal image improvement) and other miscellaneous expenses

The total cost of your start-up needs will not exceed $20,000 Canadian.

Professional/Trade Associations You May Like To Join/Know

Canadian Public Relations Society
220 Laurier Avenue West, Suite 720
Ottawa, Ontario
K1P 5Z9
Phone: 613-232-1222
Website: www.cprs.ca

International Association of Business Communicators
1 Halladie Plaza, Suite 600
San Francisco, Ca 94102
USA
Phone: 1-415-433-3400
Website: www.iabc.com

Books you May Need to Buy:

6 Steps To Free Publicity
Published by Career Press Inc.
Author: Marcia Yudkin
ISBN: 1-56414-675-8

Endless Referrals: Network Your Everyday Contacts into Sales (New and Updated Edition)
Author: Bob Burg
ISBN: 0070089973
Guerrilla Publicity
Published by Adams Media Corporation
Author: Jay Conrad Levinson, Rich Frishman, and Jill Lublin
ISBN: 1-58062-682-3

How To Become Your Own Publicist
Published by McGraw-Hill
Author: Jessica Hatchigan
ISBN:0-07-138332-8

How To Open and Operate A Home-Based Communications Business
Published by Globe Pequot Press
Author: Louann Nagy Werksma
ISBN: 1564406318

The Practice Of Public Relations
Published by Prentice-Hall
Author: Fraser Seitel
ISBN: 013613811X

Public Relations: Strategies & Tactics
Published by Addison Wesley Publishing Company
Author: Dennis L. Wilcox
ISBN: 0321015479

Effective Public Relations
Published by Prentice-Hall
Author: Scott M. Cutlipp, Allen H. Centre, and Glen M. Broom
ISBN: 0132450100

Lesley's Handbook of Public Relations and Communications
Published by NTC Business Books
Author: Phillip Lesley
ISBN: 0844232572

The Handbook Of Strategic Public Relations and Integrated Communications
Published by McGraw-Hill
Author: Clarke L. Caywood
ISBN: 0786311312

Public Relations Writing: The Essentials Of Style and Format
Published by NTC Publishing Group
Author: Thomas H. Bivins
ISBN: 0844203513

Guerrilla Selling: Unconventional Weapons and Tactics for Increasing Your Sales
Published by Houghton Mifflin
Author: Bill Gallagher, Orvel Ray Wilson and Jay Conrad Levinson
ISBN: 0395580390

Guerrilla Teleselling: New Unconventional weapons and Tactics To Sell When You Can't Be There in Person
Author: Jay Conrad Levinson, Mark S.A Smith, and Orval Ray Wilson
ISBN: 0471242799

Teleselling: A Self-Teaching Guide
Published by J. Wiley
Author: Porterfield James D
ISBN: 0471115673

Marketing/How To Get Business
Hunting for business for your public Relations Firm is about the same as searching for a job in your field. As such, you have to apply all the job search skills you have acquired over the years, customizing them to suit your present need and position.

- Cold calls to Companies, Businesses, Schools, Organizations and Events/Conference/Convention Organizers for information and interviews about who may need your services, and to provide them with reasons they may need the services of your Public-Relations Firm.
- Find out and incorporate the marketing methods and approaches of other professionals in your field into your own method and approach
- Network with other professionals who are in private practise in your professional Organization to find out who needs a plug for his expertise and practise.
- Yellow pages advertisement
- Brochure/Flyers
- Business Cards
- Create a Website
- Join Associations/Social Clubs
- Distribute gift certificates and discounted publicity packages to clients to give to their friends
- Send out publicity package offers for special days and seasons like Christmas, New year, Easter, Canada Day, Valentine's Day, etc.
- Keep in touch with your clients and call the clients who have not used your services for some time to remind them of your good services and any discounted offers available
- Call your clients - new/old/regular, weeks, months and or years after they use your services to thank them for using the services of your Public Relations firm, but above all, to ask them how they are doing and how satisfied they are with the result of the earlier publicity campaign.
- Offer a free publicity package to your regular clients for referrals - if they bring in four or more new clients
- Develop a weekly/monthly Newsletter, write in the local newspaper and or magazine giving tips on how to increase awareness through public relations. Act like the professional you are.

Good luck!

Chapter 28

PREPAID CALLING CARDS

Calling Cards are one of the easiest entry portals to the VoIP Industry.

As a prepaid calling card business owner, you will be practically buying and selling minutes of communication. Communication is old as mankind, and spoken/verbal/vocal communication is a fundamental form in the human community.

There has never been more need for communication than there is in today's globalized world, as humans try to stay in touch with family, friends and business partners.

North America (US & Canada) is one region of the world that is built on immigration and multiculturalism. Despite a small percentage of the world population, North America has the most wealth and industrial production. This has generated a great need for communication from North America to other countries around the globe and vice-versa.

You will be providing people with relatively low cost telephone calls from North America to anywhere in the global village and vice-versa, by setting up your own calling card system and selling calling cards to your customers. The cards will have authorization information, enabling your customers to place a call by dialing an access line that connects to the parent company that issued your license.

How It Works:
Sign up as an agent
Buy PIN batches at discount
Print your brand name cards
Distribute the PIN's among the cards
Sell the cards at your own value/price and in your currency
Set up an access number and a voice prompt

Address and Contact Information for Some Parent Companies/ Call Termination Companies

Telcan Inc.
90 Burnhamthorpe Road West, Suite 1004
Mississauga, Ontario
L5B 3C3
Phone: 905-804-9111

Fax: 905-804-9888
Website: www.telcan.net
General Inquiries: 1-888-6-Telcan(6835226)

Tseyva Pte Ltd.
No 21 Science Park Road
02 - 03 The Aquarius
Singapore Science Park 11
Singapore 117628
Phone: 65-6776-6005
65-682-89941
Fax: 65-6774-2459
Website: www.tseyva.com
Email: reseller@tseyva.com
info@tseyva.com
support@tseyva.com

Quicknet Technologies, Inc.
440 9th Street, Suite 100
San Francisco, CA 94103
USA.
Phone: 1-415-864-5225
Fax: 1-415- 864-8388
Website: www.quicknet.net
Email: sales@quicknet.net
info@quicknet.net

Eyebill Interactive Solutions
USA/CANADA
Head Office
60 East 42nd Street, #1166, New York
NY 10165
Phone: 1-877-649-5622
Fax: 1-484-247-2898

International Office
75 Krum popov Street
1421 Sofia, Bulgaria
Phone: 359-2-4900-456
359-2-4900-466
359-2-4900-462
Fax: 359-2-963-4211
Website: www.eyebill.net
Email: sales@eyebill.net
office@eyebill.net
support@eyebill.net

CALL TERMINATION.COM
Website: www.calltermination.com

What You need To Start-Up

- A Computer (with Internet connection)

    Use a desktop or a laptop computer with a 56k modem. Install the following software on the computer:
    - **Word processor (MS Office) -** Use this to write letters, create mailing labels, and address envelopes. In the MS Office you've got MS Word, Excel, Access, Outlook, and PowerPoint.
    - **Spreadsheet** - You can create charts and do your finances with a spreadsheet program. Use MS Excel for your spreadsheet needs.
    - **QuickBooks Pro** - With this, you can create custom invoices, compute sales, do electronic banking, pay your bills, control your inventory and payroll. Use it for all accounting and bookkeeping.
    - **Database** - Use a database program to keep records of clients, sellers, vendors and all your business contacts/links. With the database program, you can keep records of phone calls, faxes, meetings, conferences and seminars, and note time and dates of events and incidents. You may want to use MS Access, Dbase or Fox Pro for your database needs.
    - **Graphic** - Use this to create flyers, announcements newsletters and advertisements. You may want to use PageMaker, QuarkXpress and ClarisWorks for your graphic exploits.
    - **Scheduler** - Use this to manage your schedules.
- Phone, Fax, Printer, Scanner, Copier (can buy all-in-one)
- Office Furniture (including office supplies and office accessories)
- Insurance
- Fees payable to become a member in professional and or trade associations.
- Books
- Marketing/advertising cost.
- Professional Voice Prompt
- Internet Bandwidth
- Local Access Lines and numbers

Books You May Need To Buy:

Guerrilla Publicity
Published by Adams Media Corporation
Author: Jay Conrad Levinson, Rich Frishman, and Jill Lublin
ISBN: 1-58062-682-3

Marketing Without Advertising
Author: Michael Phillips, Salli Rasberry

ISBN: 0873376080

The 22 Immutable Laws of Marketing
Published by Harper Business
Author: Al Ries and Jack Trout
ISBN: 0887306667

The 22 Irrefutable Laws of Advertising
Published by John Willey and Sons
Author: Michael Newman
ISBN: 0470-82106-X

6 Steps To Free Publicity
Published by Career Press Inc
Author: Marcia Yudkin
ISBN: 1-56414-675-8

Endless Referrals: Network Your Everyday Contacts into Sales (New and Updated Edition)
Author: Bob Burg
ISBN: 0070089973

How To Become Your Own Publicist
Published by McGraw-Hill
Author: Jessica Hatchigan
ISBN: 0-07-138332-8

Guerrilla Selling: Unconventional Weapons and Tactics for Increasing Your Sales
Published by Houghton Mifflin
Author: Bill Gallagher, Orvel Ray Wilson and Jay Conrad Levinson
ISBN: 0395580390

Guerrilla Teleselling: New Unconventional weapons and Tactics To Sell When You Can't Be There in Person
Author: Jay Conrad Levinson, Mark S.A Smith, and Orval Ray Wilson
ISBN: 0471242799

How To Become A Marketing Superstar
Published by Hyperion Books
Author: Jeffrey J. Fox
ISBN: 0-7868-6824-4

Marketing/How To Get Business
- Networking
- Brochures/Flyers

- Business Cards
- Create a Website
- Promote your website to increase the number of visitors
- Word of Mouth
- Advertise in the Yellow Pages, newspapers, Magazines and Billboards
- Find out and incorporate the marketing methods and approaches of other resellers in your field into your own method and approach.
- Ensure that your system keeps track of each customer account balance
- Ensure that the customer account balance is being reduced according to service usage
- Allow access to detailed information about their call history and remaining balance.

The last three features will ensure customer satisfaction and retention

Good Luck!

Chapter 29

GENERAL BRIEF ABOUT THE TWO DOZEN BUSINESSES

The two dozen businesses you can run from your home, as discussed in this book, do not make up a definitive list of businesses you can start and run as a new or expanding business owner in Canada. Rather, they are good examples of the thousands of businesses you can run from your home. Selecting them for discussion in this book was based on:

- **Suitability for a new/expanding business owner**
- **Suitability for a professional and or skilled person**
- **Relative ease of access/launch**
- **Income Potential:** Businesses that will not bring in a steady and somewhat above average income are not included in this edition of this book. As a business owner, you merit more than ever to earn a high enough income to meet the demands and minimum standards expected of you. The two dozen businesses have the potential of limitless expansion, depending on what scale they are operated and or on what one wants.
- **Convenient to Operate from home/office:** The two dozen businesses discussed in this edition, are the businesses you can conveniently start and operate from your home, without any employees at least for the first year of operation, and without violating any zoning/community privacy and or residential regulations.
- **Non-Seasonal and Viable:** The two dozen businesses discussed here are evergreen businesses. They thrive throughout the year and in all seasons. A Toronto-based Canadian expert in home-based business who was consulted during the course of writing this book said thus: 'Depending on how you operate them, they could be immune to economic fluctuations and probably recession'.
- **Low Stress:** You have enough stress already, having been through several refusals in corporate corridors. The two dozen businesses discussed here could be operated with minimal stress.
- **Low Start-up Cost (less than $20,000 CAD)**
- **Service-based Business:** The two dozen businesses discussed here are all service-oriented businesses because a large number of new and or expanding business owners have one type of skill or another. Service-oriented business saves you money, because you won't spend lots of money buying tools,

equipment and storage. You have yourself, your skills, your expertise, and your services to market, rather than a product - relatively easy right? It is very similar to searching for a job/contract.

- **Accommodating:** Most of the two dozen businesses discussed here are extremely accommodating - any professional can pitch his/her flag and specialize in his/her area of expertise within the businesses.

However, there are many more businesses you can start from your home that are not listed in this edition. Do not despair if I did not list any business that suits your interest or aptitude. There are many books on home-based businesses. Most of the other home-based businesses that you may think of can be started and operated using similar methods and modalities as those pointed out for the two dozen home-based businesses in this book.

Chapter 30

POINTS TO CONSIDER BEFORE CHOOSING ANY OF THE TWO DOZEN BUSINESSES

- Are you resolved to, and do you believe in the business?
- Will you enjoy the act of conducting the business?
- Will you like the type of crowd and clients the business will attract to you?
- Will you be able to weather any setback and or crisis that may arise in the course of conducting the business?
- Will you be able to believe in and resolve to running the business, enjoy the act and process of conducting the business, enjoy the type of clients the business will attract to you, and be satisfied? Are you ready to remain the steadfast captain of the business during thick and thin?

When answering the questions, do not let your enthusiasm blind you to the obvious.

If your answer is yes + yes + yes + yes + yes then you are set to take off. It is that simple. Belief + Resolve + Happy indulgence + Joyful Client-Business owner relationship + Readiness for crisis management + Satisfaction = Total Success

The human community is ready for you and your business.

My sincere congratulations!

Regardless of the business you choose to start and operate, there are general requirements that any person in business must meet, and they include:

- Self-Management - As a self-employed business owner, you need control, restraint and motivation
- Time management - Manage your time skilfully. Time is money
- Money Management - Manage your in-out flow of cash skilfully
- Organized Office - Organize your office for optimum operation

Marketing/Advertising/Publicity - Whether it is Product(s), Service(s) or Expertise that requires selling, you need to market/advertise/publicize it in the market.

Advertising/Marketing/Publicity are simply the act of making a product, service or expertise known to the public with the sole intention of getting the public to buy and use it. People only buy the products and use the services and expertise they know about, hear about, read about or see around. Getting your product(s) or service(s) known to the public can be achieved through:

The newspaper, television, radio, internet, journals, magazines, Yellow Pages, signs, flyers, direct mailing, referrals, networking, brochures, business cards, door-to-door, seminars and conferences. Failure to stage a successful advertising/marketing/publicity campaign will waste the opportunity to get the public to know, hear, read about your product/service/expertise.

If you do not advertise your product, nobody will advertise it for you. And nobody can advertise your product better than yourself.

- **Newspapers/Magazines/Journals -** In the local newspaper/magazine/journal, you will find the ad hotline of the Publisher, you call the company and request to be directed to the marketing/advertisement department.
- **Television/Radio** - Call the company and request to be directed to the marketing/advertisement department.
- **Internet** - Create your own Website and use Web marketing techniques to increase traffic to the site. Promote your site.
- **Yellow Pages** - the phone company that set up your business line may help by telling you the advertising rates in the phone directory. Be sure to place your ad under the correct heading.
- **Direct Mailing** - contact the mailing list companies and buy lists of people that fit into your niche target market. In your yellow pages, go under the heading 'mailing list' and you will find list of mailing list companies.
- **Networking/Referrals** - always dispense excellent service and product(s) so that clients who have used them will refer others to you. Network with every client that comes your way. Organizations, Associations, Social clubs, Seminars and Conferences are excellent arenas to network.
- **Signs** - Signs can attract lots of clients in your area, as well as people passing by. People can also use the signs to locate you more easily.
- **Flyers/Brochures** - They contain literature and photos about your product(s) and service(s), your contact address, phones, fax, e-mail, and website address. Flyers and brochures can be mailed to your clients, or distributed in malls, seminars and conferences.
- **Business Cards** – A business card makes you look professional and serious. By giving a person your business card, you are telling him/her to remember you professionally with the card. Your business card is your mini-resume, brochure and flyer. Make a good one with the right contact address, phone, fax, e-mail and website address.

Thirty Second Self-selling

In all the sections of how to get business for all the two dozen businesses, I repeatedly wrote that finding business for your firm is pretty much like searching for a job in your field, and you must apply all the job search skills you learnt from the facilitators in the job search centre you attended. Remember the act of telling the employer about yourself in 30 seconds?

Yes you do.

Good!

Do you agree that the question 'what do you do?' is a very common question from people we are meeting for the first time?

Now imagine yourself sharing a seat in a plane, cruise ship, public transit – a city bus, tram/street car, in the stadium, conference hall, cinema, restaurant, bar/pub, or in a party and the question 'what do you do?' is directed to you. Most people answer this question without making proper use of the opportunity. People answer this question without giving a positive image about their profession either by omission or commission, but it is an opportunity to sell yourself professionally and dish out your business card.

Consider the following lines:

'These days Companies turn to information professionals for information on competitors, solutions to a specific problem, vetting an innovation, or increasing productivity. Because it is time and cost effective, and they get the exact information they need. I am an Information Broker. Here is my card'

'When most Companies, Businesses and Organizations want to recruit a professional, they seek the services of an executive search firm/headhunter because it is far less expensive and more effective than advertising in the newspapers. I am a Headhunter. You can have my card'

'It is an entrenched fact that relaxation and touch therapy is not only good for the body and the mind but also cures aches, pain and stress. I am a Massage Therapist. You may have my card'

In just thirty seconds you told your audience not only what you do, but also the advantages your business offers, and ways a prospective client may benefit from your services. You can practice saying it out loud in the privacy of your office, car, washroom, kitchen, balcony, living room, study room, etc, so that when confronted with the question 'what do you do?' It will flow smoothly.

The end point of Advertisement/Marketing/Publicity is to sell.

Selling has been described as the business of convincing a person to buy a product, service and or idea. Selling is an act, and like most acts, it can be learnt and applied to any field by any interested party.

However, there are some sacred steps to good in Sales. The steps are sacred because they have to be followed religiously to achieve the desired result. The steps include:

- Identifying your Market - This is pretty simple, you have to identify your client(s) before selling to them
- Introduction - introduce your product(s) or service(s)
- Qualify your client - Find out if he/she/they are suitable for your product/service
- Presentation - Tell all the pros of your product/service
- Close - make the sale

The following is a list of books on Marketing, Advertising and Publicity:

Guerrilla Publicity
Published by Adams Media Corporation
Author: Jay Conrad Levinson, Rich Frishman, and Jill Lublin
ISBN: 1-58062-682-3

Marketing Without Advertising
Author: Michael Phillips, Salli Rasberry
ISBN: 0873376080

The 22 Immutable Laws of Marketing
Published by Harper Business
Author: Al Ries and Jack Trout
ISBN: 0887306667

The 22 Irrefutable Laws of Advertising
Published by John Willey and Sons
Author: Michael Newman
ISBN: 0470-82106-X

6 Steps To Free Publicity
Published by Career Press Inc
Author: Marcia Yudkin
ISBN: 1-56414-675-8

Endless Referrals: Network Your Everyday Contacts into Sales (New and Updated Edition)
Author: Bob Burg
ISBN: 0070089973

How To Become Your Own Publicist
Published by McGraw-Hill
Author: Jessica Hatchigan
ISBN: 0-07-138332-8

Guerrilla Selling: Unconventional Weapons and Tactics for Increasing Your Sales
Published by Houghton Mifflin
Author: Bill Gallagher, Orvel Ray Wilson and Jay Conrad Levinson
ISBN: 0395580390

Guerrilla Teleselling: New Unconventional Weapons and Tactics To Sell When You can't Be There in Person
Author: Jay Conrad Levinson, Mark S.A Smith, and Orval Ray Wilson
ISBN: 0471242799

How To Become A Marketing Superstar
Published by Hyperion Books
Author: Jeffrey J. Fox
ISBN: 0-7868-6824-4

If you choose to run any of the two-dozen businesses from your home, remember that a business is being run from home does not make it inseparable from your family, household chores and activities around your home. Working from home can be very difficult because of distractions, and there is no boss watching over your shoulder all the time. You require lots of discipline to run your business from home. Discipline to separate working hours from family and friends.

Distractions may include children, friends, television, radio, and other household chores. Having screaming, crying, or giggling kids and barking dogs in the background while on a phone conversation with a client is very unprofessional and distracting. When on the phone with a client, keep the dogs away. Keep the children quiet and or out of the office with their baby-sitter/nanny or in the day care.

You have to run your home-based business like any business that is run from an executive office on Bay Street in Toronto, Canada or from an executive office on Wall Street in New York, USA.

Good luck!

Glossary of Terms

Chamber of Commerce - A union and or association of businesspeople in a community, region or area with a common interest geared towards improving the trade and commerce of such a community, area and or region.

Cold Call - Making contact with a company, organization and a person through telephone, email, and letter or in person, without prior introduction, invitation, or referral is called Cold Call.

Commissioned Agent - An agent who makes commission only on the sales he/she makes for the company.

Co-signer - A person that acts as a guarantor for another by jointly signing a legal document

Credit history - The history of how a person borrows and pays back his/her debts.

Direct Mailing - A publicity strategy that enlists sending information, advertisement materials, marketing, Sales pitch and flyers etc., by post directly to the targeted audience and or prospective clients.

Door-to-Door - The act of going from house to house, knocking at every door in a neighborhood, area and or region to sell, advertise and or publicize a product and or service.

Entrepreneurial Trait - The inherent quality and skill, which distinguishes a person as an entrepreneur and or a businessman.

Evergreen business - Business that thrives throughout the year and in all season.

Factoring - A type of financial service where a seller transfers a debt to another firm (the Factor) that acts as principal. The factor turns to the buyer to collect the debt. All credit card transaction is a form of factoring.

Flyer - A flyer is a sheet paper advertising products and or services.

Functional Plan - A plan that is implementable and designed to achieve the desired result.

Irrevocable Letter of Credit - This type of letter of credit, cannot be altered, amended and or cancelled by the issuing bank (the buyers bank) usually at the request of the buyer, without the consent of the beneficiary (the seller).

Letter of Credit (L/C) - It is an instrument of business transaction, a safe method of ensuring payment in a business transaction. A letter of credit is an undertaking and or guarantee for payment of a specified sum of money within a stated time frame, issued by a buyer's bank at the buyer's request. The undertaking contains conditions that must be met by the seller within a stated time frame before receiving payment.

Liability/Trouble Shooting Ability - The ability to foresee and prevent a liability and or trouble before it becomes a problem.

Line of credit - A revolving type of loan/credit, with an established maximum that the borrower may have access to, the maximum amount becomes available as soon as the borrower pays the previous borrowed amount.

Mailing Labels - Labels you can use to personalize your mailings. You can have your company logo and or mascot on your mailing labels.

Mailing List - A list of people's names and addresses in the possession of an organization, company and or a firm, used to mail information, advertising materials and or products to these individuals. One can also compile a mailing list from the phone book.

Merchant Account - An account, which enables one to accept credit card payments for goods, services and or debts.

Networking - Networking is the act of making and establishing contacts and exchanging information for the purpose of career advancement. It is the most effective tool of job searching and securing a job in Canada and elsewhere in the world. Truly, whom you know fetches you jobs much more easily than what you know.

Non-Transferable Letter of Credit - This type of letter of credit cannot be transferred to a second and third beneficiary.

People Smart - The skill and or ability to charm and deal with people in an effective and endearing way that keeps the people comfortable while doing what is required of them, and earns you their respect and or likeness.

Qualifying Examination/Test - A pass in this examination and or test qualifies one for licensing in a designated regulated profession.

Referrals - The act of referring a person and or persons to a place to obtain help, information, service and or purchase product(s).

Retainer Agent - A retainer agent is paid a fixed amount of money to work for a company/manufacturer for a particular product in a particular period of time.

Resume - A summary of your education and training, professional experience, work history, technical and soft skills, accomplishments, interests and activities/hobbies as they relate to the job position you are targeting.

Revocable Letter of Credit - A revocable letter of credit, can be altered, amended and or cancelled by the issuing bank (the buyers bank) usually at the request of the buyer, without the consent of the beneficiary (the seller).

Sales Pitch - A prepared and rehearsed speech which a salesman and or sales representative presents to the prospective buyer when trying to sell a product and or service.

Small Business Administration Act - The government of Canada supports and assists small businesses as contained in this act. The SBA provides financial, technical, advice and consulting services to small businesses.

Start-Up-Capital - The capital needed to start a business and or a venture

Success Strategy - A laid down game plan to achieve success in an endeavor

Telephone Skills - The ability and manners needed to conduct a telephone conversation / communication for the purpose of presentation, interview, research, sales, advertising and or marketing.

Term Lenders - Term lenders lend money to individuals, companies, organizations and firms for a fixed period of time, for profit.

Time Management - The act of managing ones time by allotting a task to every bit of a person's time.

Transferable Letter of Credit - This type of letter of credit can be transferred to a second and third beneficiary.

Volunteer Work - An unpaid work and or service related to your field of expertise.

About the Author

Obi Orakwue is a Biochemist, Research Associate and President of Obrake Corporation. Presently he's busy pruning his latest work entitled "Career Spouse".

His other works include:

Non-fiction
- A Complete Guide to Overcome 'No Canadian Experience': How and Where to Obtain 'Canadian Experience'
- Immigrate, Live, Work, Study and do Business in Canada

Fiction
- Corrupted Ambition
- Overqualified Labourer
- The Terrorist Creed
- Comedy of Time
- The Lost Gene
- Victim of Want

He lives in Toronto, Canada.